The Insecurity
of Everything

How Hardware Data Security is Becoming the Most Important Topic in the World

Aaron Blum | Kevin Dillon | Brendan Egan
John Shegerian | Tammy Shegerian

Names: Aaron Blum, Kevin Dillon, Brendan Egan,
           John Shegerian, Tammy Shegerian, authors
Title: The Insecurity of Everything
Subject: Cybersecurity, data destruction, electronic waste
ISBN: X

Written & Printed in The United States of America

Special considerations and thanks to Lauren Sangalis for helping make this book possible.

A special thanks to all those in our lives who have helped us both individually as well as professionally to get to where we are today.

3

Foreword by Kate Fazzini, Cybersecurity Expert & Journalist

There are few sure bets in cybersecurity. One, though, is that data needs to be destroyed.

This book is important because it tells you how, why, and what you need to know to successfully manage an enterprise's technology assets. It's also critical in conveying the understanding that cybersecurity concepts can be easy for anyone to grasp when you boil it down to this simple element: your company's most important information is on the machines that store and run your data.

When the time comes to upgrade, move, retract or expand, you have to get rid of them the right way. Here is a brief, personal look into how we got here.

Cave Etchings

It was not long after the turn of this century that I realized I had a passion for electronics. I liked dissecting them, though, not necessarily working on them.

I earned my beer, lunch, and concert money at the technology store on the campus of The Ohio State University, where I was attending college at the time. My favorite pastime was digging through the banker's boxes of discarded equipment that would sometimes flow through our store. I became a hardware nerd as I tinkered with the old, broken and malfunctioning pieces and parts, and experimented on putting them back together.

In one box on its way to the scrapyard were Apple Newtons, barely used by a university chemistry department but all in working order. I learned so much from them. I even observed how an affair between two professors unfolded on the device's rudimentary SMS feature. Texting was unheard of as a communication method in 1993. This conversation, then, was perhaps the technological age's equivalent of lurid cave drawings.

Another box held the word processors from the university's journalism program, with thousands of started, stopped, and spiked stories to read. There were research notes, business plans, personal diaries, all of the "stuff" that makes up the working world and would be multiplied many times in the coming years.

In yet another, there were servers from the university's nuclear reactor laboratory. It was like looking into Marsellus Wallace's glowing briefcase from "Pulp Fiction."

The Cuckoo

Around that time, I first read Clifford Stoll's "The Cuckoo's Egg," which is about the intrusion of East German hackers into the University of California at Berkeley's sensitive military research programs in the 1980s. It is a swashbuckling tale of technical criminal pursuit, through computers and cable boxes, wires and routers.

A Cuckoo is a brood parasite. It destroys the eggs of other birds and takes over their nests, which they've worked so hard to build. It was an apt visual metaphor then and now for the takeover of well-established networks by bad guys.

To my childish detriment, I was majoring in English, and this seemed to marry those two worlds together beautifully. It became clear to me how critically important all of this equipment would be as we mired deeper in data, and how vital it would be for institutions to do a better job of disposing of it.

Fast forward to my first corporate cybersecurity job, at JPMorgan Chase. Here, in the 2010s, I learned the term "museum piece." It was just one decade after my college computer exploits, and data had exploded. There would grow to be 100 million messages sent by SMS every day.

A museum piece at this huge corporation was basically an old computer, somehow overlooked over years of upgrades, possibly coveted by a finicky employee who only likes to use a certain model of laptop, and a comforting but old and outdated operating system.

Each of these pieces were considered a ticking time bomb. Anything that couldn't be updated to protect against the thousands of exploits constantly being developed to attack it must be. The pieces belonged in a museum, not on a desk, not in an office. If not a museum, then a shredder.

We are now nearly a decade beyond my years at JP Morgan, and again our needs have changed. Ninety percent of all the data in existence has been created since 2016, according to IBM. More people are working from home, particularly because of the COVID-19 pandemic. Scrapped equipment is counted by the tons rather than by the banker's box.

It's nearly impossible to make long-term bets on cybersecurity. The data just doesn't exist like it does for other disciplines, particularly those that involve managing disasters.

Still, there is one long-term bet that makes sense: data destruction.

Everyone needs it, whether you own common consumer electronics or you are a massive government agency. Everyone will need more of it, too, as the types of devices that store our data encompass more of our lives. Most importantly, everyone understands it, probably better than any other cybersecurity practice or concept. It's obvious and easy to explain. This last part will drive the profitability of businesses specializing in data destruction to the stars. More gadgets mean more data -- and that means more data to destroy.

Your company's computer guy

There is an old "Saturday Night Live" sketch that nails the problem of corporate technology departments. It's called "Nick Burns: Your Company's Computer Guy," who is played by Jimmy Fallon.

The recurring sketch, which aired around the same time I was working in that Ohio State computer store, has a theme song that goes: "He's going to fix your computer, then he's going to make fun of you."

It's funny, as they say, because it's true. The computer guy character uses unnecessarily technical language, insults even high-ranking executives, sighs and rolls his eyes at the luddites who don't understand him. They, in turn, despise him, don't take his advice and continue making critical errors.

This archetype exists in spades in the cybersecurity world. That's because if you don't understand the topics and the language and the lingo of this daunting and complex practice, then you need to hire a professional -- preferably the archetype -- to do it for you, at $1,000 an hour or more. This is wrong, and where John and Brendan continue to get the message so right.

A simple truth

The truth is much simpler. For most companies, having robust cybersecurity means following a well-established set of rules, many of which date back to when Cliff Stoll was chasing East Germans around the networks of U.C. Berkeley. One of those tenets is managing your assets, computers, smart phones, routers, servers and so on. And THAT means destroying them securely when they've become outdated.

This is why I love this book, and ERI. Secure data destruction is a simple concept that makes sense and genuinely moves the needle in the right direction on security. No need to speak in florid, coded language to explain it to your CEO. "You know all that important stuff you keep on your laptop? It's time to get a new one, so we're going to shred the old one securely so nobody can get what's on it." That makes sense.

And in 2021, we are sitting on piles of old smartphones, smartwatches and laptops, full of data that must eventually be destroyed for our security's sake. It's an even bigger challenge for companies that must constantly update their hardware to match the needs of the rapidly changing times. The internet of things will usher in yet more personal data -- subject to the whims of those who find it, or for corporations, the will of regulators and legislators.

We're all hardware nerds now, whether we like it or not. Listen to Aaron, Kevin, Brendan, John and Tammy, take stock of your old devices and put all that personal data in the grave for good.

Introduction by Bob Johnson, Founder National Association for Information Destruction (NAID)

I am honored to provide the introduction to this important publication, not only because I have come to admire and respect its authors and support the mission of their firm, but because the subject matter deals with one of the most important issues facing today's organizations.

While the opportunity to lend my voice to this project is personally gratifying, having dedicated a 40-year career focused on data protection, my support for this publication is also clearly aligned with the message and mission of the organization I now serve. With its beginnings going back more than three decades, non-profit watchdog i-SIGMA champions the protection of personal and proprietary information around the world, through education, regulatory advocacy, and standards development.

Emerging priorities such as diversity, equality, and sustainability have become increasingly important, not only because they are the right thing to do, but also because they dramatically impact an organization's reputation, profitability, and shareholder value.

This book concerns itself with another of those emerging priorities: privacy and personal information protection: a priority that, if neglected, causes extensive and often irreparable harm.

We live in a time when lax data security leads to devastating fines and lawsuits, embarrassing headlines, and the long-term erosion of customers loyalty, employee morale, and shareholder confidence. At the same time, privacy and data protection are the subject of a seemingly endless stream of new laws and increased regulatory scrutiny that raise the stakes even higher.

Of course, calling something a priority is one thing; making it a priority is another. As it is with anything so critical to an organization's overall health, reputation, and success, it is really only a priority when senior management make a commitment and act. When the C-suite makes it clear that shortcuts, neglect, and ignorance will not be tolerated.

In today's business climate, improper disposal of electronic media is the most misunderstood, overlooked, and vulnerable aspect of privacy and data protection in most organizations. Computer network and information protection professionals earn advanced degrees having never been exposed to the intricacies or importance of media disposition. Large organizations spending millions on cybersecurity, firewalls, training, data breach insurance, and building security, only to discard the same information they paid so much to protect with little or no regard for the security of the process or the processor selected to do so. Medium and small companies that are the least able to survive the impact of a data security breach, put their entire future at risk for the sake of expediency or to save a few cents.

Almost twenty years ago, two graduate students at the Massachusetts Institute of Technology obtained 138 discarded computers to determine what data remained on them. What they found, documented in the seminal paper *Remembrance of Data Passed*, was that the computer hard drives they obtained on the secondhand market were awash in highly personal information. This experiment has been replicated many times since, and grown in size, only to find the results have not improved. In fact, the results have gotten worse. It should be noted too, much of the personal information discovered on the original and subsequent studies was found on electronic devices previously owned by hospitals, financial institutions, defense contractors, and government offices.

In the past month, a large financial institution was fined $60 million by the U.S. Office of the Comptroller of Currency for divulging that computers recycled four years earlier may have not been properly erased. Unfortunately for them, that number may pale in comparison to settlements stemming from the class action suit from individuals put at risk by this carelessness. Once the firm learned personal information could be a risk of unauthorized disclosure, data protection laws required them to disclose the problem. Had they not, and had the potential breach been discovered later, the consequences could have been far worse.

Data Breaches & Exposed Records (United States, 2006-2020 H1)

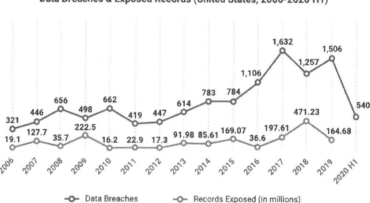

Imagine any business leader or risk manager knowing the organization's discarded electronic equipment is loose in the world with the potential it holds personal information. Imagine them knowing there are a dozen or more ways that personal information could be discovered and subsequently ruin their organization. Now imagine that there is no statute of limitations on the future data breach notification obligations, regulatory fines, and lawsuits leveled against the organization should that information be discovered in 2 years, 5 years, even 10 years. No competent risk manager or business leader knowing these facts could responsibly allow short cuts when selecting a service provider to properly protect them.

There is good news though.

First, regulators are not unreasonable. They understand there are limits to what organizations can do to protect information. The measure they expect organizations to take are logical and reasonable.

What regulators will not tolerate are organizations that ignore those basic measures. They will not tolerate inadequate or non-existent policies and procedures. They will not tolerate the absence of employee training. And they will not tolerate shortcuts in information disposal or shortcuts in the selection of service providers to destroy the information.

The second piece of good news is that, luckily, there are professionals like the authors of this book. Professionals who know their subject matter and are not afraid to tell clients what they need to hear instead of what they want to hear. Professionals who lead IT Asset Disposition firms upon which their clients can rely to do things the right way.

The fact remains, however, there is still no shortage of confusing information on the subject of I.T. asset disposal. Too often, this misinformation comes from service providers putting their own needs ahead of the clients. In other cases, it stems from clients with the best of intentions happening across outdated or irrelevant specifications.

In the end, that is why this publication is so important and, again, why I am proud to be a small part of it.

Earlier in the introduction, I referenced i-SIGMA, the international industry watchdog organization I lead. In i-

SIGMA's efforts to promote best practices in information protection, its guiding principle can be summed up as "The best way to achieve true information security is by creating well-informed clients."

A premise, as you will read, which is clearly shared by the authors and this book.

Meet The Authors

Aaron Blum

With a pivotal role in building ERI from the ground up as a co-founder, Aaron Blum has helped lead ERI to its current standing as the largest fully integrated IT and electronics asset disposition provider and cybersecurity-focused hardware destruction company in the United States. Under his stewardship, ERI now has the capacity to process more than a billion pounds of electronic waste annually at its eight certified locations, serving every zip code in the United States.

At ERI, Blum serves as the company's Chief Operating and Compliance Officer where he oversees all operations, and is directly involved with high-level sales and compliance. Blum works closely with government and regulatory agencies. He helped lead ERI's efforts to achieve the highest level of certifications available for both data destruction and responsible recycling, with all facilities certified to the following standards ISO 45001, ISO 9001, NAID, e-Stewards, and R2.

Blum has also been instrumental in the development of the corporate relations and research and development infrastructures for ERI.

Before co-founding ERI, Blum led the sales department for Pullz Computers, a Southern California-based computer resale company. Within a year of starting with Pullz, Blum helped double the company's sales revenue.

Blum graduated from the University of San Diego with a Bachelor's degree in business administration.

Kevin J. Dillon

As ERI's Co-Founder and Chief Marketing Officer and Chief Sales Officer, Kevin Dillon oversees all of ERI's corporate sales and marketing efforts, acquisitions and business development. He also sits on ERI's board of directors. With a pivotal role in building ERI from the ground up, Dillon has helped lead ERI to its current standing as the largest fully integrated IT and electronics asset disposition provider and cybersecurity-focused hardware destruction company in the United States.

Prior to ERI, Dillon worked alongside fellow ERI co-founder John Shegerian at financialaid.com to help pioneer one of the largest student loan companies in the U.S. Dillon hired and creatively managed the organization's sales force and loan counselors while growing FinancilAid.com's sales to more than $2 billion annually — leading to the organization's subsequent purchase by and transition to the oldest financial institution in the U.S.

Dillon earned a Bachelor of Science in Business Administration – Finance from California State University at Fresno, earned a certification in Cybersecurity: Managing Risk in the Information Age from Harvard University and has completed the Executive Program in Cybersecurity at MIT.

Brendan M. Egan

Brendan M. Egan is a serial entrepreneur who focuses on leveraging his experience in software development and marketing to create new technologies, disrupt existing industries, and make an impactful change in people's lives.

As founder and CEO of Simple SEO Group since 2009, Egan has advised and worked with over 300 small and mid-sized public and private companies on various marketing campaigns and software development initiatives. Egan has worked with ERI since 2013, overseeing ERI's marketing, technology, and other digital efforts. Egan also sits on ERI's Board of Directors and is the Chair of ERI's Technology Committee.

Egan is co-author of 101 Tips from the Marketing Masters: Ways to Supercharge Your Marketing & Exponentially Grow Your Business, a #1 best-seller on Amazon in the Advertising, Internet Marketing and Web Marketing categories.

Egan is also co-founder & CTO/CMO of Engage, an online platform disrupting the talent & entertainment booking industry. Egan is a partner or investor in over two dozen other software companies in the medical, financial, technology, and energy industries and serves on 8 boards.

John S. Shegerian

As co-founder and Executive Chairman of ERI, John Shegerian has played a significant role in paving the way for the electronic recycling, data protection and ITAD industries as a whole. Building ERI from the ground up, Shegerian has helped lead the company to its current standing as the largest fully integrated IT and electronics asset disposition provider and cybersecurity-focused hardware destruction company in the United States. Under his stewardship, ERI now has the capacity to process more than a billion pounds of electronic waste annually at its eight certified locations, serving every ZIP Code in the United States.

He is co-author of *101 Tips from the Marketing Masters: Ways to Supercharge Your Marketing & Exponentially Grow Your Business*, a #1 best-seller on Amazon in the Advertising, Internet Marketing and Web Marketing categories.

Shegerian earned a certification in Cybersecurity: Managing Risk in the Information Age from Harvard University and has completed the MIT Sloan Cybersecurity program.

He is also a sought-after speaker, panelist and electronic recycling, cybersecurity and ITAD industry authority. Annually he speaks across the world in Asia, Europe, the Middle East and the Americas. He has also authored articles on the industry for *Recycling Today*, *E-Scrap News* and various business journals and regularly provides his expert knowledge to news media, including *CNBC*, *BBC News*, *TIME*, *Fortune*, and *Forbes*, among others.

Shegerian also hosts *Impact with John Shegerian*, a weekly podcast featuring conversations with some of the greatest business minds and thought leaders on the planet.

In 1993 Shegerian co-founded Homeboy Tortillas and Homeboy Industries, which continues to serve as a paradigm for urban renewal in America. Shegerian is also the creator of the popular Bulldog Root Beer brand, which he launched in 1997. Shegerian then co-founded *FinancialAid.com*, filling the financial aid gap for higher education and generating one of the most successful student loan companies in the country. Shegerian founded Addicted.com in 2005, one of the largest web resources for individuals seeking help for addictions online. The website boasts a database of over 20,000 addiction centers across the United States. He is also co-founder of RecycleNation, a dynamic recycling and green living resource that simplifies the recycling process on a national level with a comprehensive, interactive recycling location database.

Shegerian is also the co-founder and CMO of The Marketing Masters, a digital marketing and web development company that builds effective, ROI-driven marketing campaigns for businesses large and small. Shegerian co-founded Som Sleep, a drink formulated to help individuals achieve better, more restorative sleep. He is also Co-founder and Chief Strategy Officer of Engage, a web-based platform designed to digitize the process of booking talent online for unique personalized appearances.

Tammy Shegerian

Tammy Shegerian oversees and manages the day-to-day operations of each aspect of the organization, including sales oversight.

It's a role she fits perfectly due to her 25 years of business management experience, most recently having served as chief operating officer and vice president of a privately held food manufacturer. For more than a decade, she was instrumental in achieving dramatic revenue growth while increasing net income through development and management of the company's continuous improvement program. During this period, the company grew from number five to number one market share in its space.

Prior to her work in food manufacturing, Shegerian served as a commercial real estate broker for Julian J. Studley (Sommer Commercial Real Estate). Focusing on office and retail leasing in the Santa Monica/West Los Angeles marketplace from 1989 to 1997, she led that firm's sales in the Santa Monica market from 1992 to 1997.

Earlier in her career, Shegerian developed her sales and sales management skills at National Service Contracts, a brokerage firm specializing in air conditioning and refrigeration service contracts nationally. Her team's sales were highest in the company and instrumental in NSC's completion of a public offering in 1989.

She started her career with the Carnation Company, working with the organization's product management program until Carnation became part of Nestlé in 1985.

Shegerian earned her Bachelor of Science in Business Administration from USC, where she graduated *magna cum laude*.

21

Chapter Overview

23

Hardware Cybersecurity & Sustainability Self-Assessment

Many companies underestimate the importance of having a sound hardware cybersecurity and sustainability plan. As you will learn throughout this book, there are a variety of laws and regulations on a local, state, national, and international level which oversee both the data privacy (cybersecurity) as well as environmental (sustainability) aspects of electronic hardware and IT assets.

In addition to various laws and regulations, the court of public opinion plans an increasing role in companies choosing to do the right thing with data security and sustainability initiatives. Irreparable damage can occur to a brand if they have just one data breach or environmental incident.

ERI has prepared a hardware cybersecurity and sustainability self-audit to assist your organization with evaluating strengths and weaknesses in your hardware and IT asset disposition plan.

We recommend you complete the self-audit prior to reading this book as well as upon completion of the book to evaluate what areas you may need assistance in improving as it relates to your hardware end of life process.

To complete this assessment, honestly answer the following questions and at the end tally up your score to see how your organization ranks.

General

1. Does your organization have a written risk mitigation strategy?
   Yes (+1)   No (+0)

2. Is your organization's written risk mitigation strategy updated at least annually?
   Yes (+1)   No (+0)

3. Is your organization's written risk mitigation strategy taught to all employees at least annually?
   Yes (+1)   No (+0)

4. Is your organization's risk mitigation strategy comprised of a defined organization with roles and responsibilities in ensuring effective implementation of security practices and measures?
   Yes (+1)   No (+0)

5. Is it comprised of critical information and hardware management from its initiation or acquisition to end of life?
   Yes (+1)   No (+0)

6. Is there a defined process to ensure effective information and hardware management from its initiation or acquisition to end of life?
   Yes (+1)   No (+0)

7. Is this process documented and auditable?
   Yes (+1)   No (+0)

8. Does it include vendor management to ensure secure Information and hardware end of life?
   Yes (+1)   No (+0)

9. Does your vendor management process include thorough qualification of Information and hardware end of life management service providers?

Yes (+1)   No (+0)

10. Does your Vendor Management include the conduct of provider assessments and audits to validate security?
Yes (+1)   No (+0)

11. Are these assessments and audits performed at a defined frequency?
Yes (+1)   No (+0)

12. Are these assessments and audits regularly reviewed against applicable and up to date processes, legislation, and contractual requirements ?
Yes (+1)   No (+0)

Sustainability

1. Does your organization currently dispose of/recycle end of life assets with a recycling provider who is e-Stewards and R2 certified?
Yes (+1)   No (+0)

2. Does your IT Asset Disposition provider offer Hardware Reuse services as Redeployment where the provider stores your equipment and redeploys it back to you at your specified time?
Yes (+1)   No (+0)

3. Does your IT Asset Disposition provider offer Hardware Reuse services as the facilitating Donation of your retired hardware to charitable institution of your choice?
Yes (+1)   No (+0)

4. Does your IT Asset Disposition provider offer Hardware Reuse services as Remarketing of your successfully data sanitized retired hardware?

Yes (+1)   No (+0)

5. Do your IT Asset Disposition provider's Remarketing services proceeds provide as revenue back to you?
   Yes (+1)   No (+0)

6. Does your IT Asset Disposition provider offer transparency on its end of life Recycling process of your hardware?
   Yes (+1)   No (+0)

7. Does your IT Asset Disposition provider promote zero landfill?
   Yes (+1)   No (+0)

8. Does your IT Asset Disposition provider rely on other downstream vendors for end of life Recycling processing of your hardware?
   Yes (+1)   No (+0)

9. Does your IT Asset Disposition provider supply a comprehensive Environmental Impact Report?
   Yes (+1)   No (+0)

10. Is your IT Asset Disposition provider active in other sustainability efforts as Environmental Legislative Compliance and Circular Economy, ?
    Yes (+1)   No (+0)

Cybersecurity

1. Does your organization currently dispose of/recycle end of life assets with a recycling provider who is NAID certified?
   Yes (+1)   No (+0)

2. Does your organization currently have a single source provider for providing asset disposition services across your entire organization (nationally and internationally)?
   Yes (+1)   No (+0)

3. Does your IT Asset Disposition provider implement secure disposition of your retired hardware?
   Yes (+1)   No (+0)

4. Does your organization's end of life/ITAD services provider guarantee secure chain of custody throughout the delivery of their services?

5. Does your organization's end of life/ITAD services provider supply you with a certificate of destruction?
   Yes (+1)   No (+0)

6. Does your organization's end of life/ITAD services provider offer you with a customer login portal that enables transparency and traceability during the entire process?
   Yes (+1)   No (+0)

7. Does your organization's end of life/ITAD services provider offer transportation services to ensure secure and safe recovery of your hardware from your chosen locations?
   Yes (+1)   No (+0)

8. Does your organization's end of life/ITAD services provider offer transportation services with Asset scanning to verify accuracy of hardware recovery from your chosen locations?
   Yes (+1)   No (+0)

9. Does your organization's end of life/ITAD services provider offer Onsite Services as Hard Drive shredding to ensure data destruction is attained prior to hardware recovery from your chosen locations?
Yes (+1)   No (+0)

10. Does your organization's end of life/ITAD services provider offer complete and transparent reporting of your retired hardware?
Yes (+1)   No (+0)

11. Can your organization's end of life/ITAD services provider provide unit level data destruction certificates?
Yes (+1)   No (+0)

12. Is your end of life/ITAD services provider's reporting easily accessible?
Yes (+1)   No (+0)

13. Is your end of life/ITAD services provider's reporting utilized to conduct assessments and audits on your end of life processes?
Yes (+1)   No (+0)

14. Does your organization conduct ITAD provider assessments and audits to validate security of its chain of custody?
Yes (+1)   No (+0)

15. Does your organization assess your ITAD provider in terms of their security compliance to applicable legislations, standards, and contractual requirements?
Yes (+1)   No (+0)

16. Does your organization's ITAD provider employ security practices that aligns to your Security Standards?
Yes (+1)   No (+0)

17. Does your organization's ITAD provider handle your service-related information at the highest level of security?
Yes (+1)   No (+0)

18. Does your organization's ITAD actively promoting Cybersecurity and upholding Privacy efforts?
Yes (+1)   No (+0)

Hardware Cybersecurity & Sustainability Self-Assessment Results

Please tally up your total self-assessment score and find guidelines below based on your results:

- **0-20:** Organizations in this range require significant changes and improvement to be compliant with best practices and ensure data security and environmental compliance.

- **21-30:** This is where most companies fall. There are ample opportunities for improvement to help ensure your organization is protected and doing the best they can with your IT assets.

- **31-39:** Overall you're doing the right things, with a few adjustments and what you'll learn through this book, your strategy can be improved and perfected!

- **40:** Great job you're doing everything right as it relates to electronic recycling and IT asset disposition!

Chapter 1: Electronic Waste: The Beginning… The Fastest Growing Solid Waste Stream in the World

The way that we use electronics has changed dramatically over the last few decades. Electronics used to be a much less prevalent commodity. It was beyond comprehension that a household would need to have more than one television set. Our grandparents had TVs that were so big they became part of their home in the same manner as a piece of furniture did. They kept their TV for 20-30 years, often until it broke, sometimes even beyond that. Eventually, professionals, or helpful relatives, would have to come in to haul these massive TVs out and inevitably toss them in the trash.

Landlines were popular and only businesspeople had cell phones. These early cell phones were massive, yet indestructible. When cell phone sizes started to shrink, they became more accessible and sought after for recreational purposes or safety reasons. Still, if you had a television or a cell phone, you had the same one for years on end. In fact, some people might still have that old phone lying around somewhere, if not for a reminder of how far things have come. One thing's for sure, back in the day no one had multiple TVs, multiple cell phones, multiple computers or screens for their computers, multiple tablets, or any of the smart technology we use now. Times have definitely changed.

In 2002, 180 million people had a cell phone[1] and very few of these were "smartphones." They weren't the pocket-sized computers we see today. In fact, the term "smartphone" wasn't used until the early '90s—hence the quotation marks. Today, it's estimated that over 5 billion people have a cell phone, many of which are the modern-day smartphones we've come to accept as normal.[2] Of these cell phone users, on average, most get a new phone every two years[5]— usually solely because they want the newest model. Things aren't being held onto simply because they still work. People are choosing to replace them because they want newer phones, faster processing chips, and better cameras.

In 2002, you probably had one TV in the family room that was shared by everyone. Today, there's an average of 2.5 televisions per household.[3] Not only that, but instead of keeping the perfectly good television set they have, people tend to upgrade their TV at least every four to five years.[4] Everyone wants the best sound system, the clearest picture, and the newest TV technology. With virtual reality coming out, even more new electronics are being created. Just like the cell phone issue, old technology isn't replaced because it's broken; it's replaced because we want something new, something better.

We're also developing new technologies every day. In 2002, going to the kitchen and opening your refrigerator was a simple act. Today, smart fridges are becoming more prevalent than ever. There are kitchen gadgets that will tell you what's in your fridge

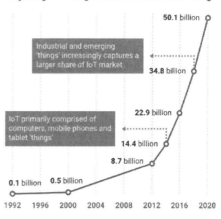

Projecting the 'Things' Behind the Internet of Things

Industrial and emerging 'things' increasingly captures a larger share of IoT market

IoT primarily comprised of computers, mobile phones and tablet 'things'

50.1 billion

34.8 billion

22.9 billion

14.4 billion

8.7 billion

0.1 billion   0.5 billion

1992   1996   2000   2004   2008   2012   2016   2020

without you having to open it. Smart devices like Google Home, Nest, Echo, Ring, and more weren't around back then, but now everyone, even children, rely on them. Nearly all adults have some sort of electronic wearables like Fitbit, Apple Watch, or other name brand fitness trackers. And many others have electronic devices that allow them to watch or play with their animals while they're at work.

While technological advancements are amazing and very welcoming in this day and age, turnover rates are faster than ever because we've commoditized all electronics. We get distracted by new products when most of them are almost identical to the ones we have in our hands. We can find new brands with the click of a button at places like Best Buy, Costco, Target, Staples, Walmart, and Amazon. To push the point further, the fees are the lowest they've ever been, and the quality is the highest it's ever been. What's even more interesting is that 51% of people have at least one unused electronic device at home, 45% have between two and five, 25% have an unused laptop somewhere, and 23% have an unused cell phone.[6] We're buying things we don't need because we want to be involved in the latest trend in technology. While that's not bad in and of itself, close to 80% of people don't have a plan to recycle any of their electronics.[6] That's an alarming number of people, considering how many excess electronics everyone has.

When the rise of technology first began in 2002, the Environmental Protection Agency (EPA) deemed electronic waste as the fastest growing waste stream in the world. The problem was that no one knew what to do with it. People would simply throw e-waste into the garbage like they do with uneaten leftovers or dirty paper towels. This created a huge problem, both for the environment and for the protection of private data. Electronic waste is difficult to break down and some of the parts create very toxic environmental results. Certain parts are valuable, while others are rare. We're running out of the natural sources of the elements we need to produce technology and they're not going to replenish themselves anytime soon. To really drive that point home, we're on track to run out of six of the elements needed to make mobile phones within the next 100 years.[6] The only way to change this is to change how we dispose of our used electronics.

To help change these dangerous, irresponsible habits of throwing away electronics, we decided to launch ERI (originally Electronic Recyclers International, Inc.). We opened our doors in 2002, shortly after the EPA said that electronic waste is the fastest-growing solid waste stream in the world. We geared up before Al Gore won an Academy Award and Nobel Peace Prize for *An Inconvenient Truth* and before there were iPads or even iPhones. Needless to say, when ERI first got into the business, it was the very beginning of a time when people and businesses started to look for ways to responsibly handle electronic waste. ERI became immersed in finding a solution and professionalized it to create a structure in terms of how to handle e-waste responsibly without harming the environment *and* while keeping personal and professional data safe. We got into the business because we thought it was both profitable and impactful and the EPA had just announced it as a proliferating problem. In ERI's first month, we recycled about 10,000 pounds of electronic waste. The next month, we recycled 20,000 pounds, the next month it was 40,000 pounds. We quickly realized we were onto something big.

Now, with eight locations nationally, we recycle anywhere from 25-30 million pounds of electronic waste a month and we're still only scratching the surface. For comparison, in 2014, the U.S. threw out about 16 billion pounds of e-waste, which is roughly equivalent to 50 pounds per every man, woman, and child in the nation.[7] We still have a long way to go to bridge the gap, but that can be understood when you consider how electronic waste has proliferated into every aspect of life. Progress is being made, but electronic waste is still the fastest growing solid waste stream in the world. The key is finding a way to address the problem in a way that's responsible for the environment and data protection. To play our part in migrating towards a circular economy and bridging the gap, all of ERI's facilities are zero waste, zero landfill, and zero emissions.

Luckily, increasing public awareness and recognition about electronic waste has made huge strides in the world. What we used to refer to as "scrap" is now called "e-waste" universally. This helps people understand the difference and thus, the fact that it needs to be handled in a responsible way. Collaboration is what will help us evolve e-waste recycling to a new, responsible level.[8] We can see this happening through the rise of the circular economy, which we'll discuss in detail in Chapter 4. This change is a result of the sustainability revolution, which is the realization that we simply don't have enough room to keep dumping things anywhere we can. We're realizing this now more than ever, so sustainability is being looked at in more detail. Local, state, and federal governments in addition to major corporations in America and around the world are banding together to find new ways to contribute to sustainability. Through a circular economy, we benefit from the reuse of products, whether it's paper, tires, plastics, or electronic waste. Throughout this book, we'll explain how this is a growing trend that's helping solve the electronic waste problem and it isn't going to slow down anytime soon.

A major contributor to an increase in electronic waste is the trend of the Internet of Things (IoT). This has been happening for a while, which is why electronic waste has been considered the fastest growing solid waste stream in the world for 18 years and counting. It describes the increased prevalence of small electronics that are infiltrating daily life in such subtle ways. Wearables are electronic waste. White goods, which used to just be considered steel scrap, now have TVs embedded in them. Nest, Google Home, Echo, Ring, and even automobiles like Tesla and Prius have computers in them. Everything is becoming compatible with the Internet of Things and we're going to continue to see this for many years to come.

Another interesting and important, factor that revolves around electronic waste is the trend of cybersecurity and the General Data Protection Regulation (GDPR). When e-waste is improperly and irresponsibly disposed of, it's easy for hackers to steal confidential, highly personal information. This has solidified the motivation to continue forward with responsible destruction of hardware, which then becomes e-waste. We **must** responsibly handle hardware and the data that's embedded in it if we want to avoid a sharp increase in cybercrimes in the coming years. Cybersecurity, or data protection, is a huge portion of this book for a reason—it's absolutely essential.

With the huge surge in people working from home as a result of COVID-19, cybersecurity is becoming an even more concerning issue. Now, previously regulated technology that was secure in the workplace is finding its way into unknown realms. It's close to impossible to monitor where remote employees use their hardware and how they secure it when they log off. This opens up an entirely new channel for cybersecurity issues and increases the risk of hardware theft or misplacement. In Chapter 17, we'll cover more information regarding the software and hardware security concerns of remote employees and their electronics.

Finally, we've been seeing 5G ads and devices pop up here and there, so we know it's coming—it's just a matter of when. The switch from 4G to 5G is going to further proliferate the amount of e-waste that we see today. This revolution in and of itself will create the biggest turnover of electronics… even bigger than when TVs transformed from black and white to color or when analog switched to digital.

Electronics started out as a small way to add convenience to our lives and have turned into a technological revolution, so it's not surprising electronic waste is *still* considered the fastest growing solid waste stream in the world. However, it's important to remember that the great inventors and innovative minds that led to this technological revolution never had malicious intent to create billions of pounds of waste. The electronic waste stream was the result of the revolution that no one really thought about. To avoid facing similar problems, we need to look at the past for an idea of how to better move forward. We can do that by making sure our e-waste goes to professionalized institutions like ERI and others who will be able to responsibly destroy it.

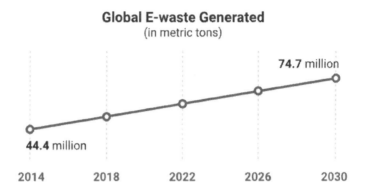

Global E-waste Generated
(in metric tons)

74.7 million

44.4 million

| 2014 | 2018 | 2022 | 2026 | 2030 |

When the EPA stated, back in 2002, that electronic waste was the fastest growing solid waste stream in the world, they probably didn't think the trend would continue. But here we are, almost 20 years later and the statement holds true. In order to make sure electronics are used responsibly, we need more stakeholders to get on board with handling e-waste in a responsible way, both from an environmental perspective and a data perspective. We need to prioritize the transformation of not only how we handle our waste, but the entire process—from design to manufacture, throughout the consumption cycle, and finally ending with the proper recycling methods. Luckily, in addition to having a great benefit on the environment and creating safer disposal of personal information, the current recycling industry is responsible for more than 531,500 jobs and an overall economic impact of nearly $110 billion.[9] It also helps to give designers feedback on products, which could have a huge impact on the future of circular economy.[9] It's just a matter of tackling it from a global scale.

Chapter 2: Electronic Waste: Environmental Protection to Data Protection and Way Beyond

Before we get into the implications of electronic waste on the environment and data security, it's important to understand what exactly classifies as electronic waste and how e-waste recycling works. Shredding a car frame is very different from shredding a computer hard drive that's filled with hazardous materials. That's why e-waste is designated as its own category.

Electronic waste, or e-waste, includes any device that has even the smallest electronic component in it. With the rise of smart technology, home automation, wearables, and smart cars, this means that e-waste is encompassing a larger sector than ever before. To make sure that e-waste is recycled properly, the electronics need to be collected and transferred to a certified e-waste recycling company. From here, individual components are removed and sorted based on their makeup—glass, plastic, or metal. Once broken down, these parts can be recycled and reused for the most efficient electronic waste processing. When done right, 100% of the commodities derived from the recycling process can be reused in a beneficial manner. However, this isn't the norm in the United States. As a whole, we handle our electronic waste irresponsibly, which leads us to two very pressing matters that need to be addressed. One revolves around environmental protection and the other involves data protection. Let's start with looking at electronic waste and the environment.

Electronic Waste and Environmental Protection

First, we want to mention something that paints the picture for how our country handles and manages electronic waste. It's disheartening to learn that a lot of e-waste recyclers in the United States market themselves as eco-friendly institutions that are dedicated to safely disposing e-waste to protect the environment

but are not living up to their word. Instead, they are shipping out e-waste to developing countries. From here, laborers immersed in poor working conditions break down the e-waste by hand, without protective safety gear or equipment. As a responsible e-waste recycling company, everyone at ERI was disappointed to learn about this. Not only are these workers putting themselves in danger, but this method was also wreaking havoc on the environment and human rights.

Thanks to the combined efforts of Greenpeace and the Basel Action Network (BAN), it is now illegal to export unwanted electronic waste, in addition to plastic waste and old ships, from North American and European countries to developing regions. However, at the time of writing this book, the United States has signed the Basel Convention, which indicates intent, but we have not actually started to follow its legal framework.[2] The United States is still taking risks when it comes to the environment.

To put this into perspective, over 134 IT and electronics recycling facilities in the U.S. have been fined, abandoned, had certifications suspended/revoked, or have been caught exporting to developing countries. Not only does this lead to disastrous outcomes, but the reputations of institutions that do this are completely squandered and many people involved now face legal action. In one example from 2018, the CEO of Stone Castle Recycling was sentenced to 12 months and one day in federal prison for the improper handling and exportation of hazardous waste, which included e-waste.[3] His actions led to the contamination of surrounding soil, causing irreparable damage to the community.

In 2018, the owners of Seattle-based Total Reclaim—Northwest's largest recycler of electronic scrap—admitted that they had collected millions of dollars from public agencies and organizations by falsely telling them that Total Reclaim was going to recycle used electronics domestically, in an environmentally safe manner.[5] This never happened. Instead, the dangerous electronic waste was shipped off to Hong Kong to be dismantled in a way that put the workers and the environment at risk.[5] In 2019, the CEO of Intercon Solutions was sentenced to federal prison for similar misguidance. Not only was he charged with wire fraud and tax evasion, but his actions also caused untold damage to the environment.[6]

While we'd hope that these kinds of bad actors would have faded with the introduction to newer, more relevant electronic waste regulations, they haven't. In January 2020, California's Department of Toxic Substances Control (DTSC) fined the recycler Freon Free for the mishandling and incineration of hazardous waste without a permit.[7] In July 2020, a lawsuit was filed against former executives of 5R Processors, an electronic waste firm in Wisconsin, for a conspiracy to store and transport hazardous waste.[8] It seems like regardless of where we turn, people continue to believe that the mishandling of electronic waste is no big deal.

So why are we one of the only countries in the world to be so reluctant to take this seriously? Because doing so leaves the United States with a problem—we don't have enough resources to take care of electronic waste ourselves. We need more people pushing for, or educated on, safe and responsible electronic recycling. We need more state and federal legislation relating to electronics recycling. At the time of this writing, there are only 25 states and the District of Columbia that have passed legislation related to electronics recycling. The rest of the country has no legislation in place whatsoever. Out of states with legislation in place, only 19 and the District of Columbia have an express landfill or disposal ban on electronic devices. That means that of the 25 states that have electronics recycling regulations, six of them can still simply throw the electronic waste in a landfill, which eliminates the whole purpose of recycling legislation. On top of everything, there are no federal laws that explicitly address e-waste recycling.[2] Simply put, electronic waste in the United States is completely out of control. We need to band together to make a stronger effort to not only understand the implications behind irresponsible electronic waste disposal, but to make a change for the better. For comparison, we're rated #25 out of the top 25 recycling countries in the world.[2] We have a problem adhering to the same environmental standards as other countries and aren't making much progress in terms of joining the movement, which is both sad and disappointing at the same time.

One of the issues at hand is that states without proper legislation are simply sending their recyclables—electronic waste included—to landfills or incinerators without any second thought. The general public continues to put their recyclables in the proper bins, but half of these recyclables are now being loaded onto trucks, taken to an incinerator, and burned.[1] For example, about 200 tons of recycling material is being sent to a large incinerator in Pennsylvania every day.[1] That's 200 tons of material that people thought they were getting rid of responsibly, which included electronic waste. What's worse is that this is happening all over the country. Most people have no idea where their old electronics are going even if they *try* to recycle.

Not only is this an unethical way for recycling institutions to operate, but it's also detrimental to our environment and the health of the surrounding people. Improperly disposing e-waste is dangerous for a number of reasons. There are countless toxic chemicals that make up the inside of electronic products. Things like lead, mercury, cadmium, copper, nickel, and zinc become harmful when they're improperly disposed of. Eventually, they release hazardous substances that make their way into the atmosphere or groundwater, therefore contaminating the air we breathe and the water we drink. When electronics are improperly disposed of, our entire ecosystem eventually gets poisoned from these hazardous materials. Long-term exposure to these types of chemicals, especially substances that have been scientifically proven as carcinogens, can lead to cancer, chronic bone weakness, pain, lead poisoning, and more. While electronic waste only constitutes a mere 2-3% of America's solid waste, the components account for roughly 70% of the hazardous material in landfills.[2]

To better understand the implications of improper waste disposal, consider the area in close proximity to the incinerators in Pennsylvania. There, the rate of ovarian cancer is 64% higher than in other parts of Pennsylvania and lung cancer rates are 24% higher.[1] What's worse is that once these toxins are saturated in our environment, it becomes difficult, if not impossible, to keep them out of the food chain. As the electronic waste problem continues to rise, people will be consuming increasingly larger amounts of harmful substances, without any knowledge of it. This doesn't happen when we responsibly recycle e-waste.

So, when we stop for a minute and consider the impact of improperly disposing of our electronic waste, it's no wonder that countries like China and Thailand have already taken their own action. They initiated bans on the importation of e-waste prior to the act passed by BAN—they were sick of taking the responsibility and undergoing the physical ramifications caused by foreign waste.

Now, the United States is at a turning point. It is our time to take action, especially if we want to avoid the situations that are plaguing developing countries as a result of simply throwing out or burning their electronic waste. Because of this, ERI has taken numerous measures to help extend our recycling efforts across the country, make the act of recycling e-waste easy and convenient, and adhere to strict eco-friendly policies that conduct responsible processing and recycling of e-waste in our designated facilities.

When all of the electronic waste issues began back in 2002, ERI took an environmental position. It wasn't yet a widely accepted position, but we saw it as a necessary step forward. Environmental action after the technological revolution was interesting to everyone. After developing all of this great, life altering technology, we slowly began to realize the mess that it made and thus, protecting the environment became a hot public topic. We realized that there was a need for an environmentally safe way to handle e-waste that never existed before. That's why we originally founded ERI. However, after a while, in 2008 or 2009, the environmental protection push kind of faded away. Some institutions wanted to do the right thing, and some didn't— not everyone was excited about the environment anymore.

As technology advanced, we realized that data protection was another critical component of the handling and disposal of e-waste. Nobody had talked about this before, but it needed to be addressed. What are we supposed to do with the growing amount of data that exists today? How do we protect our clients, their data, and the liability of being sued for improperly handling that data? This is when we started to notice an interesting trend within new institutions.

Electronic Waste and Data Protection

At this point, ERI was up and running, primarily gaining clients based on environmental appeal, but we were still paying attention. We noticed that all around us, cybersecurity companies like CyberArk and Palantir were becoming "unicorn" organizations—startups worth over a billion dollars. We also saw the rise of a company called LifeLock, which focused on privacy for consumers. So, with the concurrent rise of cybersecurity institutions and data protection firms, we realized there was more to electronic waste than we first thought. Turns out, electronic waste isn't just an environmental menace, but a cybersecurity one too.

That's why, in 2011 and 2012, we decided to start banging the drum of cybersecurity at ERI and in our industry as a whole. It wasn't received well. People thought we were crazy when we discussed our ideas about the importance of data protection through electronic recycling. Even people that were already heavily involved in the e-waste industry and e-waste recycling thought we were nuts. We moved from conference to conference trying to explain why this was so important, all to no avail.

Then, in 2017, John was sitting on a panel and Robert Hackett, the lead writer for Fortune Magazine on cybersecurity, was one of the moderators. While all of the other institutions were talking about firewalls and respective software solutions for cybersecurity, John started to enlighten the panel on hardware. No one was doing anything about the safety and security of the data left on hardware. Robert asked for John's business card and, after talking later on, was shocked that no one had considered this topic before. He published an article in Fortune Magazine about these realizations. This article, titled 'Dead But Not Forgotten', made the case for us and we never looked back.

Thankfully, this shift in attitude has put data protection and cybersecurity into place as one of the major driving forces—alongside environmental protection—of how we responsibly recycle and destroy our e-waste.

Another driving force was the realization that with all of these institutions shipping e-waste abroad, there was a huge potential for an infringement on data protection. In an increasingly digital world, this is essential, especially when viewed from a national security standpoint. Think about it. Many pieces of equipment used by men and women in service are electronic, including night vision goggles, GPS systems, and radios. If these electronics malfunction, the results can be tragic. Yet a lot of the electronics used in the armed forces have been shown to be counterfeit electronics made from parts that originated in China—likely due to a company's irresponsible e-waste recycling actions. If this hadn't been discovered, the results could have been much different. We cannot allow our electronic waste to be hacked, manipulated, or used for malicious intent. We need to take data protection seriously, especially when it comes to our hardware.

In a 2017 study, it was found that roughly 40% of devices (such as hard drives, mobile phones, and tablets) that were resold on publicly available channels contained personally identifiable information.[4] This information included credit card numbers, usernames and passwords, company information, tax details, contact information, and personal data.[4] Data breaches have started to negatively affect every industry from hospitals to financial departments, retailers and the auto industry, military personnel, and even small independent businesses. Data protection is a crucial aspect of cybersecurity from the initiation of new technology to the destruction and recycling of old devices.

There are astonishing estimates that 25% of all data breaches are caused by negligence, which includes improperly recycling the e-waste after use. Every time there's a data breach caused by human error or negligence, it costs institutions around $128 per record.[9] Unfortunately, employees still tend to be the biggest risk for cybersecurity issues. The general lack of awareness an employee has regarding what they should or shouldn't be doing, alongside the increasing number of phishing emails that are sent out, creates a disastrous mix. It's important to make sure that employees understand what they need to look for in a phishing email alongside responsibly recycling their e-waste. Responsibly recycling e-waste saves institutions money and protects not only their data, but also the data of each one of their clients. This is why ERI has committed to wiping data, removing components, breaking down items, and recycling individual parts of e-waste. We need to make a collective effort to protect our data.

There's a reason that ERI is the leading e-waste recycler in the country—we care about the environment *and* we care about protecting the data of our clients. Every year, ERI processes over 250 million pounds of e-waste for clients in retail, government, healthcare, financial services, and other leading industries. In 2019, ERI recycled and reused 160 million pounds of electronics, which helped avoid roughly 980 million pounds of CO_2 equivalent emissions, 46.1 million pounds of water emissions, 2.58 billion kilowatt hours of electricity, 11,448 garbage truck trips to the landfill, and 17 million pounds of air emissions. Every single ounce of e-waste is processed in our designated facilities in the United States, not overseas. ERI recycles electronic waste such as batteries, cell phones, copy machines, desktop computers, DVD players, keyboards, laptops, light bulbs, computer accessories, televisions, printers, fax machines, stereo equipment, white goods, wearables, and more. While we pride ourselves on our commitment to responsible e-waste recycling practices, we need other recycling organizations to make the same commitments. In 2016, the world generated over 44.7 million metric tons of e-waste. That's 13.4 pounds of e-waste per person, a huge increase over the last several years and this number isn't going to stop growing. Every year, more and more e-waste is being produced and we're estimating that by the end of 2021, over 52.2 million metric tons of e-waste will be generated annually. Oddly enough, we're at a tipping point where there are more devices that aren't in use than there are active ones. This is important, since even the smallest electronic devices create large amounts of e-waste as the technology inside becomes increasingly more complex.

In order to achieve proper environmental protection and data protection we're asking that organizations approach e-waste recycling the right way. We need more processing centers and a new outlook, such as that of a circular economy. However, these processing centers need to uphold certain standards, such as R2 and e-Stewards, to keep the environment and data safe. ERI was the first company in the world to be dual certified in R2 and e-Stewards certifications, which are some of the most notable environmental certifications in the world. There is a long list of criteria that a company must meet if they're going to successfully achieve these certifications including adhering to e-waste best practices, operating a facility that meets environmental standards, being transparent with communication to the public, and taking a pledge not to dispose e-waste in landfills or incinerators. When a company gets these certifications, they're also barred from using any type of prison labor and cannot export toxic electronic waste to poor communities. This is one reason why ERI is applauding the Basal Action Network's (BAN) global ban on hazardous waste exports to developing countries. It's our responsibility to take the necessary precautions for the future of our planet. Without laws such as these in conjunction with more forward thinking and sustainability-minded organizations, we're never going to make any progress. To achieve this goal, the first thing recycling plants need to do is get certified.

Chapter 3: The History of Data Security in the United States

The concern for data security has been around forever—way before the Internet of Things dominated our daily lives. Before the increasingly common digital paperwork, government and businesses relied on paper and good old fashion file cabinets. When they used a copier, the resulting information only appeared on the paper you walked away with. Destroying papers with sensitive information was easy and profitable. To put this into perspective, in October of 2015, Shred-It, which was the largest data destruction paper shredding company of its time, was sold to a company called Stericycle for approximately $2.3 billion. That's a lot of money for a data destruction that only focused on paper trails, which demonstrates how important data security is and how much people are willing to pay for it.

Today, data security has become an even bigger challenge. The interconnectivity of our appliances, smart devices, wearables, computers, televisions, and offices makes efficient data security harder to accomplish than ever. If you go to make a copy today, the data you copied is stored on the machine's hard drive. The same thing happens when you send a fax, write an email, download a PDF, or visit a secure website. There's a data trail that's left behind in the wake of our daily actions and many people don't even realize it. So, how can you ensure that your data stays secure when it's time to get rid of, or update, your devices? You need to destroy it properly. It doesn't matter if you're in a public or private business, if you work in healthcare or at Starbucks; data security is more difficult and yet, more important than ever.

Now, there are laws in place that demonstrate a nation-wide shift in the attitude toward data security. But how did we get here? To fully understand, we need to look at the historical process and evolution of data security in the United States, starting from the beginning.

Data security measures have been in place since as early as the 1700s when Benjamin Franklin implemented postal service privacy measures by requiring postal carriers to lock their saddle bags in transit.[4] Only once they reached the destination could they be unlocked. Over time, this has transformed and now, the National Association for Information Destruction (NAID) is in place. NAID is the entity that governs all information destruction service institutions.[5] Originally founded in 1994, it was created to put rules and regulations in place so that offline data security was strictly regulated and followed a precise procedure. NAID focuses on secure data destruction and advocates for a standard of best practices across governments and service providers as well as product, equipment, and service suppliers globally.[6] The NAID AAA Certification Program is now required in thousands of government and private service contracts and is currently held by 1,000 service providers across five continents.[6] However, it didn't start out with such success. In the early days when NAID was just an idea that complemented the Certified Document Destruction (CDD) organization, thousands of people denied needing the service.[6] NAID's competition was ignorance— secure data destruction services were not mainstream practices.[6] After years of struggling to show value, NAID was established and has continued to work towards the mission of championing for the protection of personally identifiable information, intellectual property, as well as regulatory compliance through the secure disposition of information and media in all forms by promoting customer best-practices using qualified service providers.[6] As many in the offline data security business have come to know, if someone is not NAID certified, you can't guarantee that they will keep your data secure.

As computers were introduced, the realization that data security needed to be moved to the online sector happened quickly. In 1971, we saw the birth of the first computer virus. A man named Bob Thomas of BBN Technologies co-wrote a 'virus' that moved through the Internet and gained access to people's computers.[3] This virus was seemingly harmless. All it did was generate a message that appeared saying, "I'm the creeper, catch me if you can."[3] However, it paved the way for future problems. Not long after this was unleashed, Ray Tomlinson transformed it into a self-replicating virus, which many argue was for his own personal gain to boost sales of his later-developed antivirus program called the Reaper.[3] As technology has continued to advance, the data security breaches have become more serious. The rise of cybercrime has taken over the world and now costs the global economy over $6 trillion a year. New cyberattack strategies are being developed and are more sophisticated than ever before. Increased connectivity puts more data online and the sensitive systems that we have operating on the web create more opportunity for cybercrime. Prestigious organizations have been exploited alongside the United States government itself.

"I'M THE CREEPER, CATCH ME IF YOU CAN."

To help safeguard data on computers, companies such as FireEye, CyberArk, Palantir, and LifeLock have opened and protected millions of people's data. Similarly, laws like HIPAA, HITECH, FERPA, COPPA, FTC, FACTA, FCRA, and more have expanded on an industry-based account.

The Health Insurance Portability and Accountability Act (HIPAA) is one of the most commonly referred to and recognized privacy laws in the United States. It safeguards sensitive health information and helps to regulate the use and disclosure of health information.[4] The Health Information Technology for Economic and Clinical Health Act expands on healthcare related data security. The Family Educational Rights and Privacy Act (FERPA) works to protect access to school records and control the disclosure of certain personally identifiable information.[4] The Children's Online Privacy Protection Act (COPPA) imposes requirements on websites directed toward children under 13 years old when collecting data and using it.[4] It requires parental consent. The Federal Trade Commission (FTC) has established legal authority and enforcement capabilities covering a wide range of privacy issues such as spam, certain types of advertising, spyware, file sharing and more.[4] The Fair and Accurate Credit Transactions Act (FACTA) helps to improve data security in terms of identity theft and the Fair Credit Reporting Act (FCRA) regulates credit card information and a consumer's right to access their credit reports. There are many industry-specific laws in place, but numerous organizations realize that these aren't good enough.

To demonstrate inefficiencies, consider a few major brands that have been hacked and are still struggling with data security problems. Adobe reported that hackers stole nearly three million encrypted customer credit card records plus login data for close to 153 million users.[7] Canva had 137 million user accounts jeopardized in a hack and eBay has continually been the focus of cybersecurity breaches.[7] Equifax, one of the largest credit bureaus in the U.S., suffered a breach that exposed 147.9 million consumers in 2017 and My Fitness Pal, a health and fitness app, had 150 million customer's data stolen and then put up for sale.[7] Mercy Health Hospital was breached and the hack exposed protected health information. Blue Cross Blue Shield has encountered multiple data breaches over the years and recently had an employee error that exposed the data of nearly 16,000 patients online for three months.[8] Even NASA, one of the most secure administrations in the United States has not been immune from cybersecurity problems. In 2019, it was found that a breach in NASA went undetected for 10 months and hackers made off with sensitive data relating to the agency's Mars mission.[9]

The problem is that while institutions have emerged from all of these data breaches and industry-specific laws, there has never been a federal law that requires data, as a whole, to be protected. Yet, as time moves forward and the Internet of Things continues to grow, the need for a more secure system is growing with it. In 2010 there were roughly 9.4 million detected cybersecurity incidents. In 2011, that number grew to 22.7 million and in 2015 it almost doubled reaching 59 million incidents per year. Now, in 2021, a cyberattack of devices with Internet access occurs, on average, once every 39 seconds.[1] Needless to say, data security is essential. We need safeguards in place to protect our digital information from cyberattacks, hackers, and data breaches. With no action, millions of people will continue to have their data stolen every day.

While we've come a long way, we still have a long way to go. We've evolved and created countless acts, legislation, and policies to help protect data. In addition to the industry-specific laws we mentioned earlier in this chapter, former president Barack Obama passed the Cybersecurity Act of 2015 to help strengthen the nation's cybersecurity. In 2016 the European Union took things a step further and passed the General Data Protection Regulation (GDPR). This was originated in an effort to create data protection requirements that all individuals, organizations, and institutions need to obey. Entities were given two years to put a plan in action and obey before the GDPR Enforcement began May 25, 2018. Now, under the GDPR, companies, organizations, or individuals are required to make their privacy policies straightforward and easy to understand so that people can provide educated consent. If companies, organizations, or individuals don't adhere to these measures, they'll be fined regardless of the size or scope of their industry. No one is exempt from the GDPR.

At first, the United States didn't do anything but watch. Throughout the years, there has been a lot of trouble with big corporations adhering to such a law, as it would cost them significant capital allocation. However, as data breaches continued to proliferate throughout the country, the government realized that action needed to be taken. Subsequently, in November 2018, former president Donald Trump signed into law the Cybersecurity and Infrastructure Security Agency (CISA) Act of 2018. CISA works on a national scale to defend against cyberattacks, works with the federal government to provide cybersecurity tools, and helps put in place capabilities to safeguard the '.gov' networks that support essential operations.[2] We also have the Federal Information Security Modernization Act, which is meant to protect U.S. residents from cyber threats. Unfortunately, there hasn't been a lot of follow up on these data protection measures. Thankfully, the U.S. is in process of transitioning into legislation that mirrors the GDPR, which we'll discuss in more detail in Chapter 5 and 6. Regardless, we need to start acting now by discontinuing the delay of federal legislation and state-mandated laws that revolve around data security.

We also need to remember that half of the cybersecurity battle is with our hardware. Many of the institutions working in the data security industry focus on software and malware—protecting data on someone's computer as they're using it. Almost no one worries enough about data security surrounding hardware, especially at the end of that device's life. This is where responsible electronic waste recycling comes in. ERI is currently one of the only companies in the world that does what we do at the scale which we achieve it—hardware destruction to eliminate threats of data breaches and improve data security for millions of people. ERI currently has eight strategic locations that provide a national solution for electronic recycling industries with e-waste and IT and Asset Disposition (ITAD) partners around the globe. Our unique infrastructure allows us to serve all 50 U.S. states and international clients in over 140 countries around the world. Our goal is to help the world improve their data security while eliminating the environmental impact that electronic waste has—which is why we've migrated towards a circular economy.

Chapter 4: Electronic Waste and the Rise of the Circular Economy

There are currently hundreds of different definitions of a circular economy. Businesses, professionals, corporations, researchers, and environmentalists all define it differently, but there's one thing that stands true across the board. A desire for a circular economy, on a global level, is starting to come to fruition. If you're unfamiliar with the term, you're not alone. There are millions of people who haven't been properly introduced to what a circular economy is. However, many of these same people have been exposed to one, whether they know it or not. We aim to bridge the gap between exposure and understanding, so that more people make an educated decision to contribute towards a circular economy rather than our current environmental model of a linear economy.

A circular economy is one that's restorative and regenerative. It's an economy that aims to utilize every last piece of waste that's produced throughout the design, development,

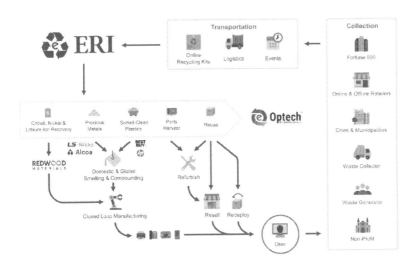

and consumption process. The idea of circularity is to make products that can come full circle; products that continue through a never-ending loop of reusing and recycling to limit the number of resources that are used and therefore exponentially decrease, if not eliminate completely, the waste that we leave behind. A circular economy aims to migrate away from the consumption of Earth's finite resources and instead use the waste we already produce in a positive way.[1] This, coupled with the use of renewable energy sources, has the capacity to completely change the way that we live and consequently, the way that the environment suffers. At the very basic level, a circular economy is what we all learned in primary school applied at a global level. The goal is to reduce, reuse, and recycle as much as possible. In doing so, we want—many would say need—to eliminate the short-term consumption lifestyles that we see today. Continuing on with our current model is unsustainable and needs to change. A circular economy compliments this change.

Not only does the idea of circularity benefit our environment, but it also creates positive society-wide benefits in the form of savings, jobs, and the increase of durable, innovative products available in the market. In regard to savings, both the business and the consumer win. A lot of big businesses and corporations think that switching to a circular economy would harm their business, but that's not the case. In a circular economy, a business won't need to spend money on new, raw materials. Instead, they'll reuse the resources already in circulation, which is far more cost effective than acquiring new ones.[2] The less money that a business spends on producing an item, the less money they'll need to charge consumers in order to make a substantial profit. This lowers the sale price, which then leads to a broader range of access for people across all income ranges. When businesses learn this, it surprises them, but the more you think about it, the more it makes sense. Have you ever considered how much money it takes to extract raw resources, transport them, break them down, and then re-manipulate them into the desired product? The manpower, energy consumption, and tools themselves don't come cheap. With circularity, the goal is to use as little as possible.

A circular economy can be seen as a system of resource utilization where reduction, reusing, and recycling prevails.[2] The goal is to minimize production to the bare minimum and when it is necessary to create something, trying to do so with elements that can be integrated back into nature.[2] This means not only switching to a mentality of reusing materials, but also re-evaluating the types of materials we begin using in the first place. In a circular economy, we'd try to use as many biodegradable products as possible. Whenever it's not possible—such as in the case of electronics—we figure out a way that we can recycle them or use them to recreate something new. Circularity strives to coincide with the natural life cycle found in nature where no waste is created, and everything has a purpose. We want to make this shift because in doing so, we'd be taking a huge stride towards a more sustainable lifestyle. "A circular economy replaces the end-of-life concept with restoration, shifts toward the use of renewable energy, eliminates the use of toxic chemicals, which impair reuse and return to the biosphere, and aims for the elimination of waste through the superior design of materials, products, systems, and business models."[3]

Biological Cycle vs. Technical Cycle

To better understand the idea of a circular economy, it's important to look at two cycles that would dominate the process of consumption. First, we have the biological cycle of things. The biological cycle encompasses all of the food or biologically based materials that can feed into the circular system through any type of composting or anaerobic digestion.[1] Put in other terms; the biological cycle is anything that aims to regenerate living things when it's broken down. This is where the design aspect comes in. We need to shift our designs to eliminate waste products that aren't biologically beneficial in order to get the most out of circularity. In doing so, the breakdown of natural materials will also lead to a production of renewable energy that can be fed back into the system to manufacture the new parts and products.

This biological cycle is then paired with a technical cycle. The technical cycle of a circular economy is about recovering and restoring the products, components, and materials of items that cannot safely be re-introduced into nature.[1] To do this, businesses will need to focus on reusing what they have, repairing what's broken, remanufacturing things that need a new purpose, or, at the very least, recycling what they don't need.

For a truly complete circular economy, these two cycles would work together using strictly renewable energy or energy created from waste products. When done right, this energy originates from each of the corresponding cycles, making the entire unit one self-functioning masterpiece that produces absolutely no waste. If implemented on a global scale, a circular economy could reduce the total annual greenhouse gas emissions tenfold and eliminate the pressure our society is putting on the environment.[4]

The Principles of Circular Economy

The idea of circularity has a number of moving parts—each of which need to work symbiotically to produce the best results. A major viewpoint of circular economy is that it encompasses seven basic principles. These include design for the future, incorporating digital technology, preserving and extending what's already made, prioritizing regenerative resources, using waste as a resource, rethinking the business model, and collaborating to create joint value.[5]

To begin, institutions need to make a shift towards future-oriented thinking. We need to stop using old design and manufacturing methods and instead, move towards researching new materials, new designs, and new ways to manufacture products that can be used for extended periods of time. We need to start designing things for the future, not the present. Next, we need to incorporate digital technology. This means we need to track and optimize resource use and work on strengthening the connections between major supply chain actors through the use of digital, online platforms and technologies that provide more insight to data.[5]

Once we begin to work through those principles, we can look at how to preserve and extend what's already been made. There's no point in throwing things away to replace them with new, future-oriented materials. We need to start recycling **now** to make the biggest impact. So, rather than simply throwing out your new phone when the newest model is released, we need to shift our mentality to see how we can give things a second life. Fix things that are broken and upgrade things that only require a small change of parts. Think about it; in the realm of things, it wouldn't be that difficult to only upgrade and replace the iPhone camera for better picture quality. Yet to accomplish this in our current model, manufacturers release an entirely new phone.

Circularity also strongly prioritizes regenerative resources—those that won't run out with time. Regenerative resources can be reused over and over, making them more preferable to finite resources that cause environmental damage. Regenerative resources are non-toxic and don't harm the Earth. When waste is created, it's then used as a resource as well. This is essentially extreme recycling—there is no waste in a circular economy that goes without purpose.

Once we get past the concept of physical resources, we need to work on reconstructing the business model. Instead of focusing on short-term consumption, we need to create greater value and align incentives through a business model that builds on interactions between products and services rather than transactions.[5] Finally, collaboration is required to create joint value between the business sector and society as a whole.

One key aspect of a circular economy is the shift of the business-to-consumer relationship. Currently, businesses sell goods to consumers and when goods run out, they need to be replaced. A circular economy would shift to a relationship that focuses more on "renting" or leasing a product rather than buying and consuming. This forces big businesses to re-evaluate the effectiveness of their products and services. It pushes them towards creating a better performing product using materials that can be recycled repeatedly and through the same consumer. What this does is replace the concept of a consumer with that of a user.[3] Over time, we could be renting everything we own rather than buying it, which would benefit the economy and reduce the number of new products that are manufactured each year.

The Rise of the Circular Economy

The beauty of these ideas is that they're already gaining popularity. A circular economy isn't something that only lives in our dreams—it's becoming a reality. 16% of American institutions are already implementing circular economy principles and 62% plan to move toward circularity in the future.[6] As institutions realize that they can actually save money by using a circular economy strategy, it shifts the stigma of what circulatory means. It's no longer *only* about saving the environment and creating a sustainable future, it's also a huge business opportunity.

Many institutions are already on the path towards circularity. Take Heineken for example. They not only recycle their glass bottles, but they also utilize the heat waste from a nearby factory to fuel their manufacturing plant, recycle the water they use, and have found a way to sell the spent grains used to make beer as an alternative cattle feed.[6] Rather than throwing out the dirty water and partially used grain, they've eliminated their biodegradable waste by contributing in a positive way. They're also working towards creating higher-value products from their spent grains by extracting proteins, fats, and other components.[6] Their goal is to eventually launch food, cosmetic, and even pharmaceutical products using this spent grain.

Dell is another company making headway. Dell has been working to design more modular technology to make it easier to recycle and refurbish computers.[6] They're also looking at how to use e-waste in other ways, such as through making jewelry from leftover pieces of a burnt-out circuit board.[6] Intel is working on figuring out how they can implement circularity into their business model and HP is reinventing the way their products are designed, manufactured, used, and recovered. HP's overall long-term and enduring ambition is to take responsibility for its products throughout the entire lifecycle—to understand and own the impacts of its products along the value chain.[7]

Adidas has officially launched shoes made out of ocean plastic and plans to stop using any new, raw plastic in its products in the near future.[6] Rothy's makes shoes from recycled water bottles and encourages recycling by offering customers free return shipping when they're ready to toss their shoes.[6] They plan to reuse the plastic from old shoes and create new products—potentially even brand-new shoes. Absolutely none of the electronics recycled at ERI are put into landfills, which eliminates electronic waste and adds to the lifecycle of products that circularity encourages.

ERI, one of the world's largest electronic recycling companies, has the capacity to shred and recycle up to one billion pounds of electronics per year so that old parts can be refurbished into new devices. By recycling electronics in a responsible way, the materials can be processed and sorted into separate commodity levels such as glass, steel, plastic, aluminum, copper, gold, silver, palladium, lead, and more. From here, these parts are audited and can be returned back into the technical cycle of materials all for beneficial reuse.

Other institutions are implementing the change from consumer to user by offering a rental service. For example, the Schiphol Airport in Amsterdam has recently signed a contract that will now use "light as a service" from a local company Signify.[6] What this means is that Signify owns the physical light bulbs, but the Schiphol Airport rents the light that's actually produced. This creates an incentive to make longer-lasting products that can easily be repaired or recycled without putting any responsibility on the consumer.[6] If this is successful, we can expect the same type of services to be rolled out with smartphones, computers, and even home appliances.

The concept of a circular economy recognizes the importance of effectiveness. It's crucial for the sustainability of both large and small businesses, organizations and individuals, and the global and local markets.[1] Switching to a circular economy helps decrease energy consumption, reduces CO_2 emissions, stops depleting finite resources, and works in favor of an effective economy. This idea has been around for hundreds of years, we just didn't have a name for it. Now, thanks to technological advances and a society that's committed to sustainability, a full-scale circular economy is on its way to becoming the norm.[6] There are still a few hurdles we'll have to get over—such as how to encourage people to send products back instead of throwing them out—but hopefully as ideas continue to develop, we'll be able to make it just as convenient to recycle a product as we are to toss it in the garbage.

Chapter 5: Electronic Waste and the Launch and Growth of the General Data Protection Regulation (GDPR)

Just as electronic waste continues to be a problem, the growing concern for privacy and regulation is plaguing the world. Over the course of four years, the European Union deliberated on developing the General Data Protection Regulation, or the GDPR, to help address these issues. A draft of the GDPR was released in January 2012, but European Parliament didn't support it until March 2014.[3] Once the votes were passed to back the GDPR, it worked its way through legislation until it was finally scheduled to be enforced in May 2018.[3] To give everyone time to adapt their privacy policies and regulations, it was announced in April 2016 that organizations would have two years to change their policies so that they would comply with the GDPR. This deadline was set for May 2018.

The goal of the GDPR was simple. The European Union wanted to standardize and strengthen data protection policies for residents and members of EU nations.[4] It went further than the outdated Data Protection Directive, more strongly met the current online needs, and was stricter in compliance. This was just the tipping point.

Millions of people living in the European Union woke up to find their inboxes flooded with emails from any organization they had previously given information to. The subject lines were all the same: there was an update in the privacy policy, and you needed to accept the changes to continue using their site.[5] While many people didn't think twice about these messages, the implications for organizations lacking compliance with the new regulations were too great to risk. The GDPR made it necessary for any company, organization, or individual who displays a privacy policy to use straightforward terms and make sure that people can understand the implication of consent. Because of this, a lot of privacy policy agreements needed to be updated.

The entire text of the GDPR includes 99 articles that aim to clearly define the rights of individuals and any obligations placed on businesses subject to the regulation.[5] These regulations extend to institutions outside the EU that are using European citizen's data. The standards outlined in the GDPR were high, and a lot of institutions needed financial help to make sure that they were in compliance.[5] However, the GDPR was necessary in an ever-growing digital world. It is a way to help protect an individual's livelihood and inherent rights as a person. As data breaches of large-scale corporations continued to grow, the GDPR became the best possible course of action in securing the future.

Included in the GDPR are two major protective rights— one of which is the right of erasure, or the right to be forgotten.[5] With this right, you can request an organization or business to remove your data from their site entirely. Under GDPR rules, the organization has to comply with your wishes and remove or erase your data. The other major protective right is the right of portability or transparency.[5] This means that when given the choice to either "opt-in" or "opt-out," the terms and conditions need to be clearly stated so that any individual can understand the subsequent consequences of their decision. Using technical jargon or language that's difficult to understand is not allowed. The data that's covered in the GDPR includes any personally identifiable information—name, address, date of birth, and social security number—any web-based data, HPPA and genetic data, biometric data, racial and/or ethnic data, political opinions, and sexual orientation.[5] Failure to comply results in hefty fines and potential closures. In addition to these rights, you have the right to be informed, the right of access, the right to rectification, the right to restrict processing, the right to object, and any rights in relation to automated decision making and profiling.[8]

If you're an organization that processes data, you have to adhere to seven different principles that cover protection and accountability. You need to maintain lawfulness, fairness, and transparency to your data subject.[8] You must process data only for legitimate purposes that were explicitly stated at the time of collection from the data subject.[8] Organizations need to collect and process *only* as much data that is absolutely necessary for whatever purpose specified.[8] You need to keep personal data accurate, up to date, and only store it for as long as necessary for the specified purpose.[8] You must only process the data in a way as to ensure appropriate security, integrity, and confidentiality and you need to uphold accountability.[8] There are strict rules as to what constitutes consent and all organizations must receive consent without coercion.

Another difference that the GDPR has brought to consumers is the right to know when their data has been hacked.[7] This allows them to secure other data, change passwords, and call any appropriate support institutions to help mitigate the damages from stolen information. Now, organizations are legally required to inform all of their consumers when any aspect of their data has been compromised. The GDPR clearly states that if a business or organization is breached, they must tell their users immediately. As a whole, the GDPR is seen as one of the toughest privacy and security laws in the world.[8]

Something that is important to understand is that the EU's GDPR applies to all organizations that are located inside of the European Union *and* all firms or organizations that are located outside of the EU that offer free or paid goods or services to EU residences or monitor the behavior or EU residents in any way.[1] That means that major corporations that are based and operate from the United States need to adhere to the rules of the GDPR when it comes to people who live and reside in the EU. Due to the increase in global business, this means that hundreds of organizations in the United States need to be compliant for the GDPR—even though it's not technically a federal law in the United States. When institutions do not comply, they're fined just as an EU company would be. Because of this, we've seen a huge shift in how the United States views the GDPR, which we'll discuss in the next chapter.

After the enforcement of the GDPR began in Europe in May 2018, the government started to fine institutions that were not adhering to the new regulations. For those that do not comply, there are penalties of up to €20 million, or 4% of their global annual turnover, whichever is higher.[5] To make sure that people understood this was serious, they focused on targeting big institutions to make examples out of them.

It's simple: if you fail to comply with the GDPR standards, you'll be hit with a lawsuit. This is exactly what happened with Facebook and Google on the day that the GDPR started enforcing their laws. Facebook ended up reaching a $5 billion settlement with the Federal Trade Commission over repeated privacy violations.[9] Google received a $57 million fine from France for violating the sweeping package of European data protection and privacy rules that attempt to reshape the way online institutions do business.[10] The lawsuit stated that both institutions coerced users into sharing their personal data by either requiring their consent to share their data or denying them access to the site.[6] This all-or-nothing option violates the GDPR's provisions that cover particularized consent.[6] Oracle and Salesforce also received lawsuits as the European non-profit foundation The Privacy Collection claimed that they breached the GDPR in relation to how they process and share personal data collected in cookies.[11] For other institutions, these lawsuits were an example of how serious enforcement was monitored.

To make sure that you avoid staggering fines, let's look at how you can ensure your organization is in full compliance with the EU's GDPR.

First, you need to understand the basics. You don't need to read the entire text of the GDPR legislation, but you should have a strong understanding on what you need to do to be compliant. You'll need to know what personal data is, what's covered, how it flows through the system, and what steps you need to take to protect this data.[2] Know the basics, best practices, guidelines, and recommendations along with who to contact if you have any questions. Then, create an inventory of your current data. This will take some time, especially for larger organizations, but it allows you to gain a better understanding of what data you have, where it came from, where it's stored, and how it's shared with any third parties.[2] Next, you need to consult consent guidelines and make sure that you know when, where, and how consent is required across your site.[2] Consider doing a data purge so that you can start with a fresh slate. Purge any data that is either no longer used or that's obsolete.[2] Finally, do some research on how to get an Article 27 representative that can be your point of contact to ensure you're adhering to the correct EU GDPR legislation.[2]

We recommend that all organizations currently operating online in any degree take these steps. Since the passage of the GDPR in May 2018, the United States has started to create similar local legislation. As the GDPR continues to rise in America, these practices are slowly becoming the norm. To get a better understanding, let's dive into the version of GDPR coming to the United States.

Chapter 6: Electronic Waste and GDPR Comes to the United States

While data security in the United States has come a long way, we're still lagging behind the curve of other developed nations. Thankfully, with the EU's passage of the GDPR, the United States has finally started to make some much-needed changes on the federal level. One of the largest shifts came when organizations in the United States realized that they were still being held accountable to the EU's GDPR if they were providing goods or services to people that lived there. As we mentioned, the EU started to fine huge corporations to make an example of them and show how serious this was. One of these institutions was Google. Google was hit with a €50 million ($57 million) fine for violating the EU's GDPR.[1] The French data privacy watchdog CNIL accused Google of a lack of transparency, providing inadequate information and lack of valid consent regarding the personalization of ads, in addition to several other alleged violations.[1] At the core of things, the GDPR enforcement team does not believe that Google provided the information that people needed about why they're using personal data, how long it's stored, or what kind of data is being used for these personalized ads.[1] Facebook also faced a fine due to repeated privacy violations, which resulted in a $5 billion settlement with the Federal Trade Commission (FTC).[2]

Not only did the EU's GDPR prompt fines, but it also led to more organizations seeking electronic waste recycling companies that are focused and committed to security. As a result, there have been a marked increase in institutions asking ERI to destroy hardware at their offices—especially when data is too sensitive to travel.[3] To help comply with these institutions, ERI will bring in trucks with mobile shredders so that the electronic waste recycling and data destruction can occur on-site under the watch of a company's security or IT team.

We saw a trend washing over the nation. With the combination of growing electronic waste problems that showed no signs of slowing down anytime soon, a lack of federal laws in the United States that required proper recycling of their electronic devices, and an increase in privacy issues and cyberattacks, small changes were made. Americans watched what other countries were doing about cybersecurity and data security and slowly, the GDPR started to make its way to America.

But why did it take so long? The Federal Information Security Management Act was signed into law in 2002 and was meant to protect United States residents from cyber threats. It was amended and renamed in 2014 to the Federal Information Security Modernization Act but kept the same rules. There have also been state laws in place to help keep your vital information safe. However, for a long time the government wasn't following these protection measures to the fullest. Institutions weren't complying and there were very few, if any, punishments. The scariest thing is that some of the agencies that were not receiving effective ratings, a.k.a., not complying, were major governmental agencies. They included the Department of Health and Human Services, the FDA, Medicare/Medicaid, and the National Institute of Health. Weaknesses were found in data protection and privacy areas, risk management, configurations, incident responses, monitoring, and planning. Real-time monitoring was lacking and despite recommendations to correct issues, a lot of institutions did nothing year after year. As time continued to pass and we saw a rise in cyberattacks, only then did people start realizing that data security was something they should start prioritizing.

One of the biggest wakeup calls was the data breach of Equifax in 2017. Over 148 million people's personal information was exposed in the breach. It included everything from social security numbers, dates of birth, driver's license information, credit card numbers, phone numbers, and more. Equifax ended up dodging fines and were simply told to improve their security. Unfortunately, this happens all the time. In 2018 large institutions such as Reddit, HealthCare.gov, Instagram, the United States Postal Service, Amazon, Marriott, Google, Facebook, Twitter, NASA, BevMo!, Blue Cross Blue Shield, and more all faced data breaches. In 2019, some of the largest breaches in history occurred. Marriott's breach affected 383 million people alone.

When we saw the European Union's passage of the GDPR, a lot of people in the United States began to speculate whether or not we'd do the same. There was some hope that it would happen, but it wasn't happening fast enough—especially when compared to the increasing rate of cyberattacks on the citizens in the U.S.

So, why exactly was there a delay?

It all came down to money. Some of the country's largest institutions like Google, Facebook, and other tech institutions make most of their money monetizing the data they collect. Thus, if consumers could block their data from being collected or stored, the institutions would lose a lot of revenue. When looked at as a societal impact, this leads to job loss and less money put back into communities across the nation. However, since the data breaches have been steadily increasing over the years and are following a pattern that indicates things will only get worse, a lot of states began taking their own action that reflects the GDPR.

Currently, all 50 states have their own data security regulations and are planning on passing versions of the GDPR to tighten the rules around data protection and privacy for governments, small institutions, and publicly traded institutions. The main problem is here is that there is no definition of personal data or even what constitutes a data breach.[5]

California has already passed new legislation along with Nevada, Maine, and New York. Close to 25 other states have introduced a comprehensive privacy bill—some of which have made a lot of progress working their way through legislation. Those states include Washington, Arizona, Nebraska, Minnesota, Wisconsin, Illinois, Mississippi, Florida, Hawaii, Virginia, Maryland, Pennsylvania, New Jersey, New York, Rhode Island, Connecticut, New Hampshire, Massachusetts, New Mexico, Texas, and North Dakota.[6] Other states have introduced limited bills. These states include Wyoming, South Dakota, Louisiana, Kentucky, South Carolina, and Vermont.[6] These laws vary from state to state, with some being more restrictive and effective than others, but we are making progress. California has added six new state legislations strengthening privacy laws and 17 others are pending carryover.[7] Connecticut has enacted a law that establishes a task force to examine the information that businesses will need to disclose regarding consumers' personal information that is retained or sold by such businesses.[7] Hawaii has updated their laws and regulations to current privacy standards and prohibits the sale or offering for sale of location data.[7] Illinois has amended the Genetic Information Privacy Act revolving around sharing or selling information acquired by genetic testing institutions and has 13 other laws currently pending.[7] Kentucky, Louisiana, Maine, Massachusetts, Maryland, Minnesota, Mississippi, Montana, North Dakota, Nevada, New Hampshire, New Jersey, New Mexico, New York Pennsylvania, Rhode Island, South Carolina, Texas, Utah,

Vermont, Washington, and Puerto Rico are among the other states currently pushing for amendments and new privacy laws.[7]

Alongside these data security regulations, at least 35 states and Puerto Rico have separate data disposal laws.[5] 14 states and Washington D.C. are currently looking at restricting how Internet service providers can collect and share consumer data and 19 states are considering amending their existing security breach laws.[5]

California has been the leading example for statewide legislation. Beginning January 1, 2020, under the California Consumer Privacy Act (CCPA), Californians will have more rights to see exactly what information a company wants to know, where that information will be sold, and if they want that information stored. Any California company that makes at least $25 million in annual revenues and makes half of their income selling personal information or store records for at least 50,000 consumers must abide by these rules. Any company that's closely linked to businesses that meet these qualifications must also comply. This law was modeled on the GDPR but has gone further to better protect the residents of California. One thing that makes the CCPA even stronger is that individuals will be allowed to file a suit against a company that has violated the CPPA.[3]

Washington passed the Washington Privacy Act (WPA) on March 6, 2019, which is also patterned after the GDPR and offers many of the same protections. The WPA goes one step further and addresses how and when facial recognition technology can be used,[3] which is phenomenal considering how fast our technology is developing. This act targets residents of Washington, but it will only apply to organizations who have at least 100,000 consumers' data or derive 50% of their revenue from data and process 25,000 consumers' data.[3] This will be enforced starting July 31, 2021.[3]

The New York Consumer Privacy Act (NYPA) is very similar to the CCPA in that it would empower individuals to inquire about what data a business has collected on them, who they share it with, and provides individuals with the opportunity to opt out of having their data shared or sold to third parties.[5] Currently the NYPA is the only U.S. data privacy law that will impose fiduciary duties on any legal entity that collects, sells, or licenses personal data.[5] It's stronger than many other state laws in that it requires each business to put their customers' privacy before their own profits.[5] This is currently pending in the state senate and if approved, businesses will have 180 days after enactment to comply.

The Massachusetts Data Privacy Law, otherwise known as the Standards for The Protection of Personal Information of Residents of the Commonwealth, was enacted in March 2010 and provides requirements that work to protect Massachusetts residents against identity theft and fraud.[5] The state of Massachusetts is currently working on a more stringent CCPA-like data privacy regulation that is slated to go into effect January 1, 2023.[5]

State-level data privacy regulations continue to grow, and existing laws are being amended to better encompass the dynamic cybersecurity landscape.[5] There have been hundreds of bills introduced between 2018 and 2021 across the United States and while many will not pass, they help set the precedent for future amendments.

In addition to statewide legislation, there are currently seven forms of the GDPR working their way through the federal legislative channels in Washington, D.C. These include the Social Media Privacy and Consumer Rights Act, the American Data Dissemination Act, the Data Breach Prevention and Compensation Act, the Consumer Online Privacy Rights Act, the Data Care Act, the Consumer Data Protection Act, and the Internet Bill of Rights.

The Social Media Privacy and Consumer Rights Act requires online platform operators to inform a user, prior to a user creating an account or otherwise using the platform, that their personal data produced during online behavior will be collected and used by the operator and third parties.[8] Every operator must provide specific and accurate information to their consumers and any violations can result in civil action in federal court.

The American Data Dissemination Act will impose privacy requirements on providers of Internet services that are similar to the requirements imposed on Federal agencies under the Privacy Act of 1974.[9]

The Data Breach Prevention and Compensation Act will establish an Office of Cybersecurity within the Federal Trade Commission (FTC) who will be responsible for supervising the data security of credit reporting agencies, including thorough annual examinations.[10] It will also require the proper notification to the FTC and relevant agencies, consumers, and the public regarding a data breach that affects a credit reporting agency.[10]

The Consumer Online Privacy Rights Act is meant to provide consumers with foundational data privacy rights, create stronger oversight mechanisms, and establish meaningful enforcement on a federal level.[11] The Data Care Act establishes duties for online service providers with respect to end user data that such providers collect and use.[12] The Consumer Data Protection Act is being introduced to protect consumers from information shared for the purpose of contact tracing with respect to COVID-19. Specifically, it prohibits covered entities from collecting, processing, or transferring an individuals' personally identifiable information for the purpose of contact tracing with respect to COVID-19.[13]

Finally, the Internet Bill of Rights includes six principles for consumers to have more control over their personal data. These rights include the right to universal web access, the right to net neutrality, the right to be free from warrantless metadata collection, the right to disclose amount, nature, and dates of secret government data requests, the right to be fully informed of scope of data use, and the right to be informed when there is a change of control over data.[14]

With these changes, we're going to have Federal GDPR and state-by-state GDPR, which will tighten the noose and create more legal actions against the bad actors that misappropriate their constituent or client data. As long as these laws include strong enforcement provisions, such as the effective enforcement and fining of the EU's GDPR, we should start to see a shift in how our data is kept secure.

A lot of organizations are wondering what these changes would mean to their operation. Unfortunately, for many organizations that rely on selling personal information, a lot of changes will need to be made. To help prepare, you should start moving away from purchased lists and instead try to engage your visitors enough so that they want to leave their information willingly. You'll need to change how you use opt-in forms and try to determine how you can give your visitors value instead of spammy content. Be more transparent with your brand and on an internal level, do a complete assessment of your current cybersecurity measures in place.

It's refreshing to see this progress. We've made some great strides regarding data security and federal and state legislation, but there's still work that needs to be done—especially concerning electronic waste. Cybersecurity, the protection of sensitive data, and electronic waste all work together—they encompass parts of a whole. To work toward the benefits of a circular economy, we need to reward manufacturers for designing better products. Starting from the chain of production is the only way to make this shift a long-term reality. The more recyclable a product is, the easier it will fit into a circular economy model and the less likely the waste is to fall into the wrong hands. We need more state and federal laws to make electronic recycling mandatory. While the advancement of the GDPR in the United States has started to pave this road, we're not all the way there yet. Giving manufacturers the power to choose which devices they collect to recycle doesn't work in the interest of the whole; it only works in the interest of the manufacturer. Finally, all stakeholders need to think long-term.

While there is a lot of new legislation in place for laws that mirror the GDPR, most of them don't mention electronic waste. The laws that do discuss electronic waste only mention that customers need to mail in their unwanted electronic devices to the manufacturer if they want to participate in recycling programs. That's a lot of effort for the average consumer and the way it's set up now is pretty inconvenient. The best way to solve this problem would be implementing permanent recycling facilities so that we could have collection services or secure drop-off sites similar to what ERI is doing in New York. ERI has increased accessibility to electronic recycling to over one million New Yorkers by implementing on-site pickup for electronic items along with free recycling services. The more convenient recycling is for the average consumer, the more likely they will do it.

We should launch awareness campaigns about the dangers of sending e-waste to landfills so that people get a better understanding of why this is so important. This way, even if the legislation fails, conscientious people will still be able to make a decision based on their perspective regarding the protection of the environment and their own data—many of which would do so simply for environmental interests alone.

As we previously mentioned, if you want to take matters into your own hands, there are a few best practices that can be implemented within institutions without privacy compliance staff. First, take the time to learn the basics. By having a solid foundation of information about the GDPR, you'll be able to migrate through your day-to-day tasks with a better understanding of privacy compliance. That's not to say we recommend reading the GDPR text in its entirety, but there are a few guidelines, recommendations, and best practices you should be familiar with.[4] Next, take the time to go through and inventory your data so that you understand exactly what it consists of, how much of it you have, and what actually qualifies as "personal data."[4] Once you have a better understanding of what your data consists of, consult the consent guidelines to understand whether or not you need to reach out and actually obtain consent for how you're using the personal data of your consumers.[4] If you have any questions regarding consent under the GDPR, spend some time on their website researching the guidelines for consent. If you don't think you can obtain consent, or if your consumers don't grant you it, then it's time to enact a data purge policy.[4] Make sure that you adhere to any requests that fall under the right to be forgotten and move forward with new data by utilizing best practices. Finally, for all future interactions, it's best to get an Article 27 rep that can help you with communication regarding local data privacy laws and compliance.[4]

The past few years have documented some of the largest breaches in history, and we're hoping that the legislation state and federal governments are taking in 2021 and beyond will help us to prepare for the future. However, with the rise of the Internet of Things, we speculate that the target is going to switch to devices. Since things like video security cameras, wireless sensors, smart speakers, wearables, and other smart technology all transmit data, we need to make sure and prepare ourselves for cyber threats on these devices. Hackers can access the information and use it against us or steal our private information. We need to either disconnect these items from the Internet or take stronger security measures.

Another thing we need to prepare for is the shift from 4G networks to 5G networks. This shift is meant to drastically increase the speed of which data is transmitted, thus increasing the speed at which data theft can be committed. We need to stay one step ahead, but it's going to be challenging. We need federal and state legislation in addition to businesses having a secure team in place to prevent and monitor breaches. For now, you can take actions to help safeguard your information or—if you're a business—protect your customers and comply with the up-and-coming laws. As a consumer, never share your data with an unsecure site or network and always make sure you understand what you're consenting to. As an organization, work on being more transparent and make sure that you can prove that what you're doing complies with the laws. For both consumers and organizations, take the proper precautions when recycling your electronics by using a recycling company that you can trust.

Always look for an e-Stewards certification and ensure that the company has the R2 Standard certification as well as NAID for data destruction. ERI takes responsible recycling seriously and processes all of our e-waste in the United States.

Chapter 7: The Explosion of the Internet of Things (IoT)... Is This the Beginning of the End?

The Internet has been around for decades. Since the early 80's people have been increasingly relying on it and we haven't shown any signs of slowing down. In fact, the opposite is true. We used to watch television shows like *The Jetsons* and movies like Disney Channel's *Smart House*, which gave us a glimpse of the potential of such technology. Today, these automated features are a reality. For many people, automated features have come to be an indispensable part of life. We're starting to rely on the Internet for more things than we even realize and with the rise of the Internet of Things (IoT), it's never been easier. Add in the increase in accessibility of broadband Internet, reduced connectivity costs, and faster development of smart technology and we see more people opting for devices that have Wi-Fi—regardless of what they are. Since the explosion of the Internet of Things, this seems to include an increasingly disproportionate number of items.

The Internet of Things is a description of the transformation of electronic devices that we've seen in the past decade. The concept essentially describes how nearly everything that turns on is now an electronic with connectivity capabilities. Seriously, almost every single device that you can turn on these days can be connected to the Internet and/or to other devices. This used to only mean cell phones, but it's now reached devices that we never even imagined possible. Think about what you use every day. How many of them can be connected to the Internet or programmed? The rise of the Internet of Things now includes things like wearables, headphones, kitchen appliances, smart refrigerators, light bulbs, thermostats like Nest, lamps, virtual assistants like Alexa, video doorbells like Ring, security systems, automobiles, and even children's toys, baby monitors, and clothes. Using small sensors, businesses are even incorporating items with digital intelligence capabilities. It connects all of the things we own with the Internet—thus, the Internet of Things.

It's estimated that by the end of 2021, there will be over 26 billion connected devices.[1] All of these devices collect and share information with each other and associated businesses. The explosion of the Internet of Things is making a smarter, more responsive world that merges our physical world with the digital one.[2] The two largest sectors that we see increasing within the

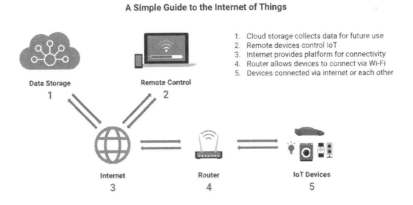

A Simple Guide to the Internet of Things

1. Cloud storage collects data for future use
2. Remote devices control IoT
3. Internet provides platform for connectivity
4. Router allows devices to connect via Wi-Fi
5. Devices connected via internet or each other

Data Storage
1

Remote Control
2

Internet
3

Router
4

IoT Devices
5

Internet of Things are utilities and security. Automation, automotive, and healthcare connectivity are projected to be the next biggest uses of IoT devices.[2]

This increase in connectivity is both intriguing and terrifying. When you connect all of your devices and a smartphone, you'll have remote access to your home, car, and even appliances inside your home. With the ability to program these devices, your car GPS could automatically reroute you to get places faster and could even send text alerts if you get stuck in traffic. Your lights could slowly start to wake you up in the morning based on your sleep cycle tracked by a wearable device rather than needing to rely on a loud and disruptive alarm. The opportunities are absolutely endless, and this is what makes the IoT so intriguing. Smart toothbrushes allow you to better understand how your brushing routine is affecting your oral health and whether or not you're missing spots, brushing too hard, or not brushing for long enough. Smart wearable devices tell you when you're most active, what your vitals are during a workout, and how well you sleep throughout the night. Smart cars can program directions, detours, self-drive, and include voice activation through connecting your cell phones. Smart homes can lock your doors when you leave or when you approach, adjust the lighting throughout the day, and record video when motion is detected. Smart refrigerators or ovens have the capabilities to track information about what you eat and when. This information can be combined with other pieces of information to create a surprisingly accurate description of who you are. IoT also has the potential to benefit businesses and how they understand their products, performance, and customer feedback. This leads to more efficient products that last longer, use less resources to produce, and can be recycled more efficiently.

On the contrary, the more connectivity that we live with, the more chances there will be for data breaches and hackers. The amount of data that is going to be collected by organizations or businesses will increase tenfold as the IoT continues to grow, making it difficult to store, track, and analyze along the way. In conjunction with more data are more security threats. The sensors that are being used on the smart technology, especially those for security and in-home automation, carry sensitive information. Unfortunately, the security of the Internet of Things has not proven to be strong enough to fully trust this revolution. Because of this, and the potential for smart devices to completely reinvent our lives, many people are wondering if the Internet of Things will be our undoing—the beginning of the end.

This is a reasonable thought. The more we rely on smart devices and interconnectivity, the more we'll demand these conveniences and the data in which they create. The more we demand, the greater risk we're at for cyber threats. We might get lazy, or we could use it to our benefit. If the Wi-Fi goes down, and all of our devices are rendered useless, will people start to panic or just resort back to life before the IoT? We don't know what's going to happen as the digital and physical world continue to merge, however the issue of security needs to be addressed.

There are numerous software flaws, patching problems, and holes in the line of connectivity throughout the Internet of Things such as with routers and webcams.[2] Due to these security flaws, hackers are starting to target IoT devices more aggressively than business websites or applications. This further begs the issue of privacy and data security. How comfortable would you be if you knew that your security system could be hacked, unlocked, or manipulated either while you're gone or worse, while you're inside? Take for example the Desoto County mother who had her family's Ring camera hacked in her child's room. While the mother did confess that she did not set up the two-factor authentication that was prompted when making a Ring account, it shows the potential for data breaches when security measures aren't fully taken.[4] Once a hacker gets inside a home's Internet grid, switching from one seemingly harmless device like the refrigerator to the security system is easy.

Similar occurrences have occurred with smart TVs. Since many smart TVs are equipped with a camera and microphone, it's important to take certain precautions. You should also keep in mind that smart TVs track data. Many people aren't aware of this and thus, don't put any security guards in place. However, we need to start treating our IoT devices like our computer systems—with as many security measures in place as possible.

Now, even the FBI is warning people about their smart TV's security.[8] Smart TV's come with a camera, a microphone, and are connected to the Internet for access to streaming apps, gaming, and digital recordings. The FBI has warned people looking to buy the newest Smart TV that they can grant access for hackers to enter your home through a backdoor to your more personal, secure technologies.[8] Not only can they gain control of your microphone or camera to watch and listen in, but they can also travel from the unsecured Smart TV network to access your locked and encrypted computer.[8] This puts nearly every home with a TV at risk and we need to take more action to ensure they're secure.

Your smart car is also at risk. Since most new automobiles are basically huge computers on wheels, your car is vulnerable to hackers. Depending on the technological capabilities of your smart car, hackers could do everything from access the information to exploit sensitive material or take over complete control of your car—from the steering wheel to the gas pedals and brakes.[7] While we don't like to think about why someone would do that to an average civilian, it's possible and the more convenient technology we add, the more likely it is to become a reality. The average car has over 150 million lines of computer code—some even more than a Boeing 787.[7] This means there are a lot of vulnerabilities and opportunities for cyberattacks.

All of these instances and more have caused a lot of concern across both state and federal government, which is another reason we need to work on cybersecurity techniques.

Unfortunately, cyber protections seem to lag behind growth when it comes to connected devices.[5] Because of the complexity and vastness of smart devices and the IoT as a whole, many hackers have realized that these devices are an easy target. Now, hackers are focused on designing malware to compromise IoT devices. In fact, about 70% of malware activity monitored by Nokia Corp.'s Threat Intelligence Lab is related to targeting connected devices.[5]

Data breaches have been steadily increasing year after year in conjunction with the increase of smart devices and stagnant security laws. As we continue to grow in the IoT, data starts to overflow. There's too much data to protect. Right now, there are around 11 billion devices connected to the Internet and that number is only going to keep growing. By the end of 2021, it's projected that there will be 26 billion connected devices and by 2025, 80 billion. This increase in devices leads to more data, which makes it harder and harder to protect everything.

Smart devices pose massive data security threats not only because of the amount of data that they create, but also because of the way that data is accessed, shared, and encrypted. Many devices use weak passwords, unencrypted communications, and insecure web interfaces.[3] This makes it even easier for hackers to access data and steal it or use it for malicious activity.

This idea is easily applied to businesses as well. The more automated a business is and the higher number of smart devices that become connected, the more ports of entry open up for access. Remote access of devices in a business industry could lead to even more serious data breaches than we've seen in the past.

While many people can understand the explosion of the Internet of Things on small-scale levels, a lot of people don't realize what these implications could mean. We know what our smartphones can do and how we can program Alexa or Google Assistant to basically run our entire household and we understand how smart technology can help advance our business, but what about on a larger scale? Smart cities are on the rise and more states are taking on this initiative to better understand the environment and their residents.

We've also seen the Industrial Internet of Things (IIoT), which is the same concept as consumer IoT devices, just on an industrial scale. The goal of IIoT devices is to use a combination of sensors, wireless networks, data, AI, and analytics to measure and optimize industrial processes.[2] This revolution could help to increase overall productivity in the workforce and save millions of dollars, but there's one thing that we have to remember. The more things are becoming connected to the Internet, the more electronic waste is being produced.

When electronic waste isn't properly disposed of, there's an even bigger cause for concern. As we've discussed, hardware still contains information that hackers can use to steal or compromise sensitive information. In the past, people thought of hardware as old computers, phones, tablets, or other smart devices. Now, hardware covers a much vaster category of things. With the Internet of Things, anything that has a sensor or switch, that can be turned on or off, or that can be connected to the Internet is considered hardware. With 63% of organizations facing security breaches due to hardware vulnerabilities,[6] we need to change the way we handle our hardware when we're done using it. Rather than simply throwing away an old TV or donating it we need to make sure that a reputable electronic waste recycling plant is processing it. If we don't, we're going to continue to compromise our data and be the victim of cyberattacks.

The Internet of Things is not the beginning of the end; it's really the end of the beginning. The Internet of Things is prompting a new-age technological revolution and electronic waste is the backside of it. It wouldn't be surprising if the Internet of Things evolved into the Internet of Everything and when that happens, we need to be prepared for the consequences. It's time to make some changes beginning with stronger security and ending with the proper electronic waste recycling protocols. We believe that working toward a circular economy is one of the only ways to reduce the environmental, health, and societal impact of the ever-evolving Internet of Things.

Chapter 8: Smarter Cities, Dumber Practices: The Massive Need to Secure the Data of the Cities and Their Constituents

As the Internet of Things continued to expand, ERI realized that this technological movement wasn't going to fade away anytime soon. As we said at the end of the previous chapter, the Internet of Things is not the beginning of the end; it's really the end of the beginning. It's the end of the beginning of the technological revolution. Now we're shifting into a more in-depth, middle ground where everything is becoming digitalized and accessible on the grid of connectivity. Every time new technology is released, people become overwhelmed with the advancements and often wonder how it's going to get any crazier than this. Then, since the technologies become weaved into our daily lives, we get used to things until the next big advancement. Well, get ready because the technological revolution is just getting started.

In addition to the extreme proliferation of the Internet of Things, we're seeing a shift toward smart cities. IoT is making this easier by saturating the marketplace with items embedded with sensors and Wi-Fi capabilities. In conjunction, Artificial Intelligence (AI) technologies are being implemented to help manage resources of smart cities and provide solutions to ongoing efficiency or security problems. In only a few short years, politicians have started to rely on the increasing data at their disposal to tackle the problems they're facing in their cities.[1] The reality of it is that smart cities have made life easier, both for residents and for city officials and they aren't slowing down. It's predicted that smart cities are going to grow significantly in upcoming years—from $308 billion in 2018 to $717.2 billion by 2023.[5]

Smart cities can help regulate air pollution emissions, detect fires, monitor soil moisture, manage incoming shipments, control perimeter access to non-authorized areas, keep track of radiation levels, check for water leakages, control water quality, or detect rubbish levels on streets.[2] They can detect where any smartphone user is, how traffic congestion moves throughout the day, or monitor parking space availability across a city.[2] Sound monitoring technology can track noise throughout a neighborhood, smart lighting can active street lights whenever needed, and smart roads can transmit warning messages or suggested diversions according to certain conditions like accidents or traffic jams.[2] The opportunities for reducing overall waste and improving the efficiency of the city's infrastructure are endless and we've only just started to scratch the surface. With the capabilities to connect this data to smartphones, residents can easily monitor problems and get real-time updates of any relevant information. There are also algorithms being developed that can work with city information to provide predictive analysis on a number of things such as fire risk, health inspection improvements, and more.[3] Not surprisingly, in the cities where these algorithms were implemented, the data has helped cities to become more efficient.

The thing we have to remember is that to achieve a smart city, we need to use a lot of technology. Sensors are put on everything from water pipes, electric meters, and parking meters, to roads, lights, sidewalks, or traffic poles.[3] These sensors help cities gain a better idea of what's happening in real-time so they can communicate the information back to the residents or to city officials for future improvements. In Louisville, Kentucky, there have been 1,000 sensor-equipped inhalers distributed to asthma sufferers to better map where the city's air quality triggers breathing problems.[3] Mobile data such as this has also advanced efforts to clean streets, track overly crowded areas, and get direct feedback from residents in a streamlined way. Infrastructures like bridges, roadways, and railways can be monitored using sensors to update structural changes like potholes, cracks, or ice.[4] All of this is great, but again, it requires technology.

The more technology that's used, the more we need to focus on the pressing concern for cybersecurity and push for more stringent enforcement laws. The smarter that cities become, the more data that they'll collect from their residents. The more data there is, the greater the concern for privacy. When paired with hundreds of thousands of sensors, video surveillance, and audio capabilities, this can get serious fast. If officials want to take on the challenges of being a smart city, they have to create smarter practices. Unfortunately, a lot of cities are moving forward without doing this first. Instead, they're still using inefficient security practices. According to officials and security experts, the current defenses are unlikely to keep hackers at bay, especially as cities become increasingly smarter.[6]

The more connections that are created throughout and across devices, the more vulnerabilities there are in the system. Hackers will have more access, and more opportunity, to steal valuable inforamtion.[6] There are a few ways that we can make changes, but they need to happen quickly. One way that experts recommend adapting cyber defense is by reducing the reliance on passwords in favor of identifying specific devices to a network.[6] This would mean that the sensors work with cybersecurity rather than against it, but this needs to be implemented from a manufacturer level. Hopefully, as the federal legislation mimicking the GDPR moves through the legal process, we start to see a shift towards stronger cybersecurity practices. If not, we could face cyberattacks on the nation's electric grid, which would be debilitating. If the electric grid were to be attacked, criminal groups or terrorists could gain access to sensitive information, industrial control systems, distribution networks, or worse.[7]

With the rise of smart cities, it's no surprise that a lot of practices are becoming increasingly dumb. We're moving toward a world of automation, and the excitement of these changes puts security on the backburners. But we can't let them stay there. We need to make sure that our priorities are in the right place. While this is a very serious matter in terms of security, another thing we need to be conscious of during this shift is the increase in electronic waste that will be created.

ERI recognized this as a possibility when we started to see the rise of electronic waste back in 2002. We saw a trend in the consumerism of these devices and, as we suspected, it's exponentially increased ever since. While it's interesting to marvel at the newest edition of the iPhone, sit and speculate on how digital clothing could make choosing your outfits and accessorizing easier and more enjoyable, or enjoy the conveniences of smart cities, electronic waste is still a major drawback.

Electronic waste is going to continue to exponentially increase alongside the release of these products and the growth of smart cities. ERI currently manages electronic waste for about 400 cities in the United States, including major metropolitan areas such as New York City and Los Angeles, that are under contract and use our electronic waste recycling services. In the beginning, when we started in this industry, we had to talk to politicians in order to get them on board with using our services. If they were more on the progressive side, they were really into what we were doing from an environmental standpoint because they knew that their constituents, or at least some of them, cared about this. If they were on the conservative side, they were less interested in environmental factors and more interested in the possibility of job creation. While everyone was encouraging, it took a little time to get both sides on board.

Eventually, all of the politicians we were talking to realized that it's good to be green. Their constituents responded to this and younger generations were more likely to back them when they supported environmentally green initiatives. Now, it's just good politics to be green, regardless of your party. Because of this, we've seen a rise in cities getting on board with ERI's electronic waste recycling program and other legislation that revolves around electronic waste. However, with the rise of the Internet of Things, this electronic waste is starting to encompass more and more of our daily lives. With smart cities, this electronic waste grows exponentially, and most politicians aren't aware of these implications.

Why exactly are we talking about electronic waste recycling programs and politicians? Because the Internet of Things is beginning to encompass entire cities. Now, many politicians seem to be in some sort of race to be the most advanced, the greenest, and the cleanest. But with the rise of smarter cities, these politicians are taking on foolish practices. Corners are being cut and information isn't being digested enough for people to understand the implications of their actions. This includes the process of recycling electronic waste. So unfortunately, dumber practices becoming second nature. There's a lack of understanding about the proper way that electronic waste needs to be handled and some cities still just don't get it. Instead, their residents continue to toss their old iPhones or computers into the recycling bin with plastic, paper, and glass.

Luckily, other cities are paving the way. Los Angeles and New York are examples of smarter cities with smarter practices. While New York officials originally said that they were never going to have an e-waste program, ERI came up with a solution they couldn't pass up. Since 2013, New York has been working with ERI to responsibly recycle electronic waste. Now, over 8,000 buildings in New York have ERI's proprietary recycling bins and it's the most successful residential and municipal e-waste recycling program in the world. Due to ERI's recycling practices, this ensures that all of the resident's data is properly destroyed before being recycled to protect the privacy of its residents. Since we recycle 100% of the electronics we collect, data destruction is essential. If people can be successful with their electronic waste recycling in New York, people can be successful with electronic waste recycling everywhere.

Moving forward, it's important to look at each city on a case-by-case basis. Some cities don't have the infrastructure to have their own e-waste recycling plants like New York does. Instead, we need to adapt and transform. One way to do this is to allow people to come to city hall or another public area to recycle their e-waste. The city can collect this e-waste for their residents and work with institutions like ERI to get it to the appropriate facility. ERI also has programs that can work with consumers living outside of the vicinity of electronic waste recycling plants. We've started to implement a mail-back box service as a solution for recycling kits in Los Angeles alongside with our safe center drop-off locations. Our kits include the box, shipping labels, and sealing supplies along with return postage to the nearest ERI facility. These recycling kits come in 19 unique options depending on the individual or industrial need. Not only does this help take care of the electronic waste problem, but it also helps keep constituent data secure by guaranteeing the hard drive or sensors don't end up in the wrong hands. Remember, there's still a huge need for responsible hardware data destruction, which we'll talk about in the following chapter.

Chapter 9: The Growth of the Cybersecurity Era and the Forgotten Need for Responsible Hardware Data Destruction . . . The Dirty Little Secret of the Privacy and Data Protection Industry

In Chapter 2, we discussed data protection and the importance of making sure that you're covered. We want to revisit this idea for a minute and pick apart data protection in a little more detail. If you recall, we talked about the rise of data protection in the form of software solutions. As soon as we emerged into the digital age, software cybersecurity companies were sprouting up left and right to help protect the information that was actively being stored and manipulated on the computer. As a response, cybersecurity unicorns become more prevalent. People understood the need to protect their data while they were actively using a device or service.

Throughout the United States, companies such as Tanium, Netskope, Kaseya, Verkada, Cybereason, SentinelOne, Lookout, Illumio, and more are ranked as some of the top unicorns in the industry—a private company is valued at over $1 billion. All of these cybersecurity unicorns aim to do the same thing; protect your data on your software. This means while you're actively using it. Software solutions are a huge part of cybersecurity, but despite what many people think, they're not the complete picture. While software solutions aim to lock the front door and the garage, they still leave the hardware backdoor open. That's where hardware solutions like ERI's come in.

Hardware solutions ensure that after you're done with technology, the data that's kept on the device is completely wiped and destroyed prior to the physical electronic being recycled or reused. If you're spending millions of dollars per year on software solutions then proceed to misappropriate your hardware, you might as well have not wasted the money. You're still leaving the door wide open. Unfortunately, this happens more often than you'd think. Institutions don't realize the need for responsible hardware data destruction, and this ends up coming back and haunting them in many ways.

Results from a recent survey show that 80% of all enterprises were found to have a stockpile of about 400,000 units of unused equipment stored away, waiting to be cleansed.[4] That's 400,000 pieces of hardware that could be hacked and have data stolen from. Due to a company's internal processing time, these devices could sit for weeks before anything happened. Without regulations in place for responsible hardware data destruction, these institutions are putting their information at risk to the same degree as if they weren't using any software data protection programs. In fact, roughly 63% of organizations have faced at least one security breach due to hardware vulnerabilities in the last year.[5] The problem is that when it comes to hardware breaches, it can be difficult, if not impossible, to track the source. Because of this, we often never get the full story behind hardware breaches.

When looking at the impact of the second-hand IT market on data protection, studies have found that almost 42% of 159 hard drives purchased online still held sensitive data.[6] Out of these drives, 15% contained personally identifiable information, despite the seller indicating that they had properly wiped the hardware.[6] While not everyone who receives second-hand IT equipment will use the data for malicious intent, you never know when it will land in the wrong hands. Unfortunately, deleting data off of hardware can be difficult if you don't know what you're doing and simply destroying it doesn't guarantee that you're safe either. This isn't the first time we've seen this. In 2016, a similar analysis of 200 hard drives bought online showed that 67% of them had personally identifiable information.[7] That's why professional hardware data destruction is so important.

According to the largest study conducted to-date by the National Association for Information Destruction (NAID), the presence of personally identifiable information on electronic devices sold in second hand markets remains high.[10] Close to 40% of all devices resold have been shown to contain sensitive, personally identifiable information including credit card information, contact information, personal and company data, tax details, and more.[10] 40% is a huge number, especially when millions of hardware is recycled or re-sold every year. The majority of the hardware that had sensitive information included cell phones, tablets, and hard drives.

Similarly, when hardware ends up in developing countries, we've seen high accounts of data breaches. Hundreds of pieces of hardware sent to developing countries to be "recycled" still have sensitive information on them because the company responsible for processing didn't bother to use proper data destruction methods. If someone has your old hard drive and it wasn't properly wiped, it's very easy to extract information like credit card numbers, passport information, online transactions, and other intimate details of a person's life.[8] In Ghana, a piece of hardware was found that had a $22 million government contract on it, which included sensitive information, and this isn't a rare occurrence there.[8]

While we don't tend to hear about hardware data breaches as often as software breaches, they do happen. In 2006, four hard drives sold on eBay that contained hundreds of thousands of confidential documents, employee names, social security numbers, and confidential memos to the CEO of an Idaho Power Company were accessed.[9] A computer at Loyola

University that held information for roughly 5,800 students was thrown out without being properly wiped.[9] Even photocopiers with Internet capabilities are at risk. Photocopiers that were used to copy sensitive medical information were sent to be resold without having the hard drives wiped, only to be discovered later in a warehouse.[9] This raises the problem that people don't think about the hardware in their electronic devices outside of smartphones or computers.

However, with the rise of the Internet of Things, more and more consumer products are becoming hackable. In October 2016, major websites like Netflix, Twitter, Reddit, and even The New York Times were inaccessible for several hours due to a vulnerability that was found in potentially millions of devices such as webcams and digital video recorders.[12] It was believed that these devices were going to be used to hack into dozens of secure websites, which is why they were out of service for hours. Malicious actors can use unsecured hardware to get inside of a network and access more secure software making the Internet of Things a dangerous network of interconnected, loosely secured hardware. This can translate to identity danger as well as physical danger, as we will see when discussing the instance where a Jeep Cherokee was hacked so that they could take over control of the car in Chapter 15.

The Internet of Things was projected to include 200 billion smart devices which communicate wirelessly by the end of 2020.[13] By 2021, more than half a billion wearable devices alone will be sold worldwide—all with interconnectivity capabilities.[13] It was projected that by the end of 2020, nearly 90% of new automobiles would be online.[13] What does this show us? The opportunity for cyberattacks are increasing and if we don't responsibly recycle our hardware when we're done with it, or when it's time for an upgrade, this data is going to fall into the wrong hands.

It's important to note that even with cybersecurity measures in place for software, data breaches are still happening. Major institutions are still falling victim to data breaches and cyberattacks—many of which cost an average of $1.1 million.[2] Yet hundreds of institutions have admitted that they've failed to keep accurate inventories of both hardware and software.[11]

Instead of letting these data breaches continue, IT needs to expand its focus from protection only to "protection, detection, and recovery."[1] While cybersecurity programs for software exist, organizations still need to go the extra mile so that they can detect threats in a timely manner. To take it one step further, hardware data destruction needs to be included in part of the cybersecurity plan. If it's not, then we're going to continue to see data breaches well into the future and they're only going to get worse. For now, to try and mitigate the biggest cause for cybersecurity issues—human error—many insurance companies are rolling out cyber insurance policies.[3] Unfortunately, these policies can only attempt to help offset the cost of data breaches—they can't do anything to reverse the breach from having happened.

Chapter 10: Fed up with the Feds: Why Even the Federal Government Hasn't Figured Out How to Protect Our Data or Privacy Yet

We discuss the issue of data security in more than a few chapters throughout the book for a reason. We're fed up with the federal government and the lack of initiative that's being shown. The transition towards legislation mirrored after the GDPR is a good step, but it's still in the process of being passed into law. We're behind the curve. While there are a number of state laws in place for data disposal, there is no federal e-waste disposition policy that acts as an overall, overarching structure. Instead, they allow each agency, or state, to do their own thing. This isn't good enough.

Many major institutions like Google, Facebook, Apple, Amazon, Twitter, Airbnb, and more have supported the move towards federal laws aimed at protecting user privacy.[1] They believe that doing this will help keep things uniform across the nation so that institutions that do business on a larger scale won't have to deal with scrutinizing every state law and changing their infrastructure to a per-case model. If they continue to operate like this, things will get messy and could lead to more vulnerabilities across data security. To keep things consistent and ensure that security is covering all vulnerabilities, this federal legislation needs to include e-waste disposal laws. Any organization that's not carefully disposing their outdated electronics is adding to the problem of data breaches, but without a more consistent law, there are loopholes that institutions can jump through to cut costs and bypass state laws.

In the past 10 years, data breaches have led to close to 4 billion records being stolen and right now, federal cybersecurity is still just as vulnerable as public and private corporations. In

October 2018, the Pentagon's Vulnerability Disclose Program processed thousands of loopholes in the Department of Defense's website.[2] In one instance, a teenager named Jack Cable found that the Department of Defense's secure filing system had a vulnerability known as an "insecure direct object reference," which involves brute forcing reference numbers into a URL to access different files without the need for authentication.[2] While this was luckily not exploited, it shows how easy it would be to access and use this information by someone with malicious intent.

This instance wasn't the first or last of its kind. In 2017 alone, federal agencies reported 35,277 cyber incidents.[3] Regardless of the advancements in data security around the world, our federal agencies continue to fail at implementing basic cybersecurity practices and leave classified, personal, and sensitive information vulnerable to theft or security breaches.[3] One of the most concerning aspects of this is the sheer number of hardware that has been misplaced or lost. Agencies are failing to keep accurate inventories of their hardware and therefore, can't track things if they go missing. This has been a consistent problem for the past decade in agencies such as the Department of State, Department of Transportation, Department of Housing and Urban Development, Department of Health and Human Services, and the Social Security Administration.[3] It's time to change the outdated systems being used and bring in more secure processes that give guidelines regarding creation, repairs, and destruction of both hardware and software. We need to look at the complete process of the supply chain—from creation to destruction.

In a discussion of major institutions like Facebook, Google, Amazon, Apple, and others with U.S. lawmakers, there were some suggestions made about how to craft new data privacy rules. These institutions support the federal laws that are aimed at protecting user privacy but notice details that have been overlooked.[1] Transparency, control, access, portability, data security, accountability, and current state laws need to be re-examined. They recommend there should be a national standard that preempts the patchwork of different data breach and privacy laws across the states and countries should adopt privacy regulations that avoid overlapping, inconsistent, or conflicting rules.[1] This national standard needs to include federal e-waste processes for the best protection against cyber threats. It's truly pointless to worry about hackers and data breaches gaining access to our software if we don't protect the hardware side of things.

To get a better understanding of the importance of addressing hardware vulnerabilities throughout the supply chain, we can review the 2015 instance of Chinese spy infiltration. In 2015, a third-party security company was testing technology for some Amazon Web Services software from an external source called Elemental Technologies.[4] During their surveillance, the security company found a tiny microchip, roughly the size of a grain of rice, that wasn't meant to be there. This was reported to U.S. authorities so more information could be determined. It turns out that this chip was inserted at factories that were run by manufacturing subcontractors in China in an attempt to create a doorway into any network it was installed on.[4] So many people focus on software hacks, but hardware hacks are terrifying. They're more difficult to pull off, but when it happens, they can be substantially more devastating—especially if they go undetected.[4] This is even scarier to think about when you realize that China makes about 75% of the world's mobile phones and 90% of all PCs.[4] Since this has happened, there is still no commercially viable way for institutions or organizations to detect hardware attacks like this, nor does it look like there will be any emerging at any time soon.[4] The reason for such a lack of development is the time and money it takes to evaluate each piece of technology.

When the supply chain gets hacked, it means that products or services are infiltrated at the time of creation. The instance that occurred from Chinese infiltration above affected over 30 U.S. institutions. These types of hardware attacks undermine the federal security control that's currently in place and it brings light to a scary realization: it's nearly impossible to find a malicious chip on a motherboard once it's been created.[5] This should remind everyone that the technology industry does not have strong enough mechanisms for preventing or catching hardware supply chain attacks and we need to take action to fix it.[5] While the solution won't come overnight, it's more important than ever to do what we can to protect the rest of the supply chain such as when technology is in use and how it's destroyed.

When we look at what the federal government has done to protect our data and privacy with technology that's in use, it's not much better. In fact, due to recent events, more businesses and governments in the United States have become the target of aggressive attacks by Iranian and Chinese hackers than we've seen in years.[6] Security experts anticipate that this increase in attacks is, at least in part, a response to former president Trump's withdrawal from the Iran nuclear deal in 2018 and recent trade conflicts with China.[6] Rather than moving forward, we're seeing massive backward strides in cybersecurity. Today, we're battling increasingly sophisticated, government-affiliated hackers from China and Iran who, as it would seem, are attempting to steal trade and military secrets.[6] What's worse is that during the time of peace, it appears that Iranian and Chinese hackers have substantially improved their skills and become better at covering their tracks.[6] All the while, the United States has failed to make any progress on cybersecurity or data protection.

Cyber criminals are also getting more aggressive in their attempts to hack hardware. In 2018, we saw a Chinese woman arrested after trying to gain access to former president Trump's private Mar-a-Lago club with a USB drive that contained self-executing code.[7] After examining the USB, it appears that it held an AutoRun code that would have allowed malware to take over a machine as soon as it was plugged in.[7] These efforts were thwarted, but they show us how easy it is for things to take a wrong turn.

We've also seen how cybersecurity threats affect private and publicly owned corporations as well as government entities time and time again. The numerous instances outlined in this book strengthen our awareness of the need for the federal government to take data security and privacy more seriously. While there are a number of laws that are currently being discussed, the federal government still doesn't have a good e-waste disposition policy as an overall, overarching guideline for our nation. Instead, they allow each agency or state to do their own thing. This results in one of three things. Institutions either stockpile old electronics without properly wiping them first, institutions allow their employees to sell old electronics on sites like Craigslist or eBay, or institutions opt for "free" recycling pickup from scrap yards or recycling institutions claiming to have a responsible disposal process. In reality, and this is a very important point to remember, there is no such thing as free recycling—both on the environmental side of things and on the data destruction side of things.

With everything that we've grown to understand about cybersecurity and the importance of data protection, it's shocking to find out that a large number of federal agencies are failing to sufficiently track their electronic waste. What's even worse is that a large amount of this e-waste is still being disposed of through public or online auctions.[8] The e-waste is usually sold to a first layer contractor who promises to handle it appropriately, but then turns to subcontractors to move around hardware and different parts as they see fit.[8] This is terrible for the environment, as many of these subcontractors turn to incinerators or landfills to scrap the e-waste, but it's also a threat to national security. Improperly disposing hardware creates a huge gap in data protection that needs to be eliminated.

Many institutions feel that electronic waste is too expensive, so to avoid impacting the environment, they simply stockpile their old electronics. They store millions of products in warehouses for years on end—which, in some respects is considered illegal.[8] For starters, this runs the risk of environmental decay over time. Electronics will start to break down and once the breakdown processes reach a certain point, harmful toxins and chemicals will leak out and wreak havoc on the surroundings. In other instances, the longer an electronic device is left lying around, the more likely it is to become subject to theft. At California State University in Fresno, thieves stole an external hard drive and when this information was realized, it was determined that as many as 15,000 people could be affected from it. While the hard drive hadn't been in use for years, California State University hadn't gotten around to recycling it or destroying the data and as a result, thousands of people's data ranging from 2003-2014 was put at risk.

Another thing that continues to blow our minds is when we hear of institutions letting their employees sell their old corporate electronics on Craigslist or eBay. There have been countless instances of this turning out badly. An IT firm in

Minnesota worked with Blancco Technology Group in a study of data security. Together, they purchased several hard drives off of eBay in several countries and after analyzing the hard drives, personal data was found on almost half of them. When the sellers were contacted, they had assured the buyers that they had taken necessary steps to remove or destroy the data on the hard drives they sold. Rapid7 also discovered more than 360,000 files in a $650 purchase of 85 refurbished electronic devices like laptops, memory cards, flash drives, and cell phones. Out of the 85 bought, only two of the devices had no recoverable data—the rest were packed with personal information. Even more, only a basic search was done on these devices instead of the recommended forensic-level search. University of Hertfordshire purchased 100 SD and micro-SD cards from second-hand stores, eBay, and auction sites and found that they were able to retrieve materials like passport scans, pornographic images, emails, resumes, and more with little to no effort. Out of the 100 purchased, 66 came back with information.

McAfee's identity theft specialist purchased 30 electronic devices over the Internet and found personal information on more than half of them. He then took the effort to reach out to the sellers and let them know what he found. In response, the sellers were shocked. Every single one of them thought that they had  completely erased their data. This just goes to show you that while you might think you know what you're doing, hardware destruction is a specialized process that needs to be carried out by professionals with experience.

This gets even more serious when we consider the implications on national security. In March 2020, a used laptop that was recently purchased by a German cybersecurity firm realized that the laptop was more than met the eye. The hard drive on this laptop did not have any encryption or even password protection security features.[9] What they found was a confidential user manual and schematics for a surface-to-air missile system that is still currently in use by Germany's air force.[9] While the laptop was old, the system that was described is still in use. It's what Germany uses to protect ground troops from bombers and helicopters.[9] It's not hard to see how detrimental that could have been, but it's not uncommon. While no one knows exactly how the computer ended up on eBay, the seller of the computer said that they've recently sold 15 other laptops that were very similar to the one with the confidential information on German systems.[9] Aside from that, the reseller account said that the company sells up to 20 laptops a month, most of which are much more recent models.[9] Imagine how many of these laptops could have serious, or extremely sensitive information on them.

Another issue is lost computers, electronics, and other media. In 2017, a USB stick with 2.5 GB worth of Heathrow Airport's security records was found in the street. This was just sitting in the street for anyone to come and pick up. How this happened is still unknown, but when institutions allow their employees to take old electronics home, you can never be sure what the outcome will be.

Unfortunately, when institutions get bids from responsible companies like ERI for $0.50/lb - $0.60/lb to recycle electronics responsibly and destroy the data, many turn the other way. They call scrap yards and when the scrapyards say they can drive over to their facility, pick up their electronic waste, and recycle it for free, they don't hesitate to jump on board.

However, and we can't stress this point enough, there is no such thing as free recycling both from an environmental standpoint and a data destruction standpoint. From an environmental standpoint, "free" recycling leads to an increase in environmental exposure to toxins, which leads to substantial health effects as well as illegal dumping and offshore recycling. From a data destruction standpoint, non-certified recycling plants or scrap yards neither know how to wipe a hard drive nor do they have the resources or time to do so. Instead, they pick up your electronic waste, bring it back to their warehouse, put it into a container, and sell it via containers to the highest bidder around the world.

When old technology and e-waste is sold to private institutions without wiping sensitive data, personally identifiable information is immediately put at risk. To understand how serious this is, we want to highlight an instance in 2012 when John and the leadership team at ERI were reminded of the importance of doing what we do—responsible data destruction and electronic waste recycling.

In 2012, John got a phone call while sitting at his desk. His receptionist let him know that there was a gentleman on the phone for him and when John asked who it was or where they were from, she responded that it was the FBI and Homeland Security. It didn't take John long to pick up the receiver. The gentleman on the other line said that he was interested in visiting with John to talk about cybersecurity issues. He came in and gave John and the rest of the leadership team at ERI a lesson that discussed how historically (back in 2001, 2002, and 2003), when old electronics were purchased via containers through a seller in America, it was typically being purchased by someone in China or other developing nations. At that time, they were interested in harvesting the precious metals from old technologies so they could be smelted and resold, which was profitable. The agent continued to explain how, while this still happens, things have taken a shift. Now, when the FBI tracks e-waste containers, they've found a massive rise in people purchasing them for adverse interests to the United States' Homeland Security. People are buying the old electronics, regardless of if they're from the federal government, publicly traded corporations, or private ones, and pulling the data out of these electronics to reverse engineer the information and see what they could find. After this, they toss, burn, or destroy the remaining hardware and abandon it in deserts or rivers or forests or oceans—wherever they could. It no longer had anything to do with precious metals. Instead, it's becoming a malicious attempt to infiltrate sensitive information. Now, while this was a pretty scary thing to hear from an FBI agent/Homeland Security officer, it wasn't surprising to many people at ERI. We've understood the implications of improper data destruction for years, which is why we do what we do. However, it showed us that it was still a continuing issue that revolved around both environmental protection and data protection. Not to mention, the practices for extraction and the subsequent destruction methods in developing nations were killing countless numbers of people.

Even with China passing their waste importation laws, they're still getting information in other ways. One of which is through technological upgrades. Chinese entities are able to access sensitive information when institutions try to upgrade servers, workstations, or networking gear via outsourcing.[10]

If your company needs to send your hardware off-site to be fixed or upgraded, it's time to consider other strategies. This is especially true in terms of the federal government. In one particular breach that happened in 2009, United States military veterans had information put at risk. The federal government sent off a hard drive to be repaired without first destroying the data on the hard drive, which contained information about 76 million vets. When the hard drive was found to be irreparable, it was again sent off without anyone destroying the data. It's believed that the 76 million records were never accessed, but it's hard to be sure. In another story, a stolen computer at the Veteran Affairs Department put the records of 26.5 million military vets and personnel at risk. The original lawsuits requested $1,000 per person or $26.5 billion. This further demonstrates the concerns that remain over the lack of following recommended data destruction procedures on a federal level. Remember, it's truly pointless worrying about hackers breaking into our systems if we're willingly giving away access to our data to anyone with a website saying they're a refurbishing or repair businesses.[10]

Unfortunately, e-waste legislation regularly disappears in Congress.[12] In 2019, the Secure E-Waste Export and Recycling Act (SEERA) was introduced with plenty of sponsors on both the Republican and Democratic sides.[12] The bill focused on limiting the types of electronics that could be exported to developing countries to reduce the chances of hardware infiltration from improperly wiped electronics.[12] In an effort to eliminate threats of national security from improperly exported and recycled electronics, SEERA was great in theory. It also allowed for the potential creation of jobs in the U.S. However, eventually, SEERA was allowed to die and is now just sitting with the house's Foreign Affairs Committee.[12] Similarly, while the U.S. used to be a leader in hazardous waste, we've slowly backed away from this title. The Basel Convention was a multilateral government agreement negotiated in the late 1980s that discussed the international movement of hazardous waste.[12] It was put in place to track and reduce the movements of hazardous waste between developed and developing nations.[12]

As of 2018, 186 countries and the European Union have ratified this and follow the legal framework, but the United States has not done so—despite the fact that we've signed the Basel Convention, which indicates an *intent* to ratify.[12] Unfortunately, due to corruption, "mislabeling", and extremely lax prosecution efforts, hazardous e-waste is still being shipped from the U.S. to developing nations.[12]

While there have been *some* advancements in e-waste exportation laws from the federal government, we're hoping to see many more emerge in the future. Federal laws still don't explicitly address e-waste recycling[12], which means we have a lot of work to do. While China has banned the importation of electronic waste from developed nations, other countries like Thailand, Malaysia, and Indonesia have picked up the slack. We need to start taking this seriously, on both a local and federal level, if we're going to diminish the risk of data breaches. Luckily, we're starting to see more people facing legal repercussions of breaking these laws. There are a number of instances where people or organizations have shipped their electronic waste offshore, caused irreparable damage, got caught, and have thus ended up with fines and/or in federal prison because of it.

It's important to keep in mind that as the Internet of Things continues to grow, these vulnerable systems will extend to include much more than phones and computers. Hackers could start to derive information from discorded or resold smart TVs, doorbell services, used security systems, and even things like refrigerators or clothing. Smart homes are becoming a treasure trove of the most intimate data about your life and there are very few federal controls over it.[11] We need to consider the implications of irresponsibly recycling medical equipment from hospitals, POS systems, projectors, handheld scanners, office phones, and more. To make sure your data is being completely destroyed, it's important to work with reputable companies like ERI that will ensure that data destruction is done properly. Institutions also need to do their due diligence prior to doing business with third-party vendors. While the federal government might not know exactly how to protect our data or privacy yet, we can still do our parts in keeping sensitive information safe and secure.

Chapter 11: Healthcare and Data Protection: It Isn't Hip to Just be HIPAA Compliant

With the emerging technology and consistent technological advances, our lives are getting both easier and more complicated at the same time. We have the ability to transfer data at the touch of a finger, but the process of this transfer leaves our private information susceptible to hackers and cyberattacks. Interconnectivity is a great leap forward, but it creates a substantial risk—especially when dealing with sensitive information about a person's finances, identity, and health. For this reason, the United States has laid out a few safeguards, one of them being HIPAA.

HIPAA compliance isn't anything new. It's been around for years as a way to protect patients and their sensitive information. As soon as we started to see a shift towards digital healthcare processing and data storage, it was quickly realized that medical information needed a safeguard. Thus, in 1996, HIPAA was created.[1] HIPAA, which stands for the Health Insurance Portability and Accountability Act, outlines the standards for how to handle and protect sensitive patient data.[2] It states that any company that deals with protected health information (PHI) must have physical, network, and process security measures in place and follow them.[2] These standards are applied to any entity working in treatment, payment, or operations in healthcare as well as business associates, which are considered anyone who has access to patient information and provides support in treatment, payment, or operations.[2] At the very basic level, anyone who has professional access to medical information needs to follow HIPAA compliance.

To further increase these security measures, HIPAA has been extended to include three subsequent rules. The HIPAA

Privacy Rule covers the "use and disclosure of protected health information (PHI) and the standards that must be upheld for individuals to understand and control how their individually identifiable health information is used by an organization."[1] It applies to health plans, health care clearinghouses, and providers that conduct certain health care transactions electronically.[3] It works to prioritize patients' rights over their health information, including rights to examine and obtain a copy of their health records and to request any corrections.[3] Finally, the HIPAA Privacy Rule requires appropriate safeguards to protect the privacy of personal health information and therefore sets limits and conditions on the uses and disclosures that may be made of such information without patient authorization.[3]

The HIPAA Security Rule outlines the security standards that need to be taken to help protect any electronic protected health information (ePHI).[1] The only difference between ePHI and PHI is that ePHI is strictly electronically based.[1] The security standards set in place by the HIPAA Security Rule include details on technical safeguards, physical safeguards, and administrative safeguards.[1] It aims to provide added protection for information that is transferred or stored electronically, which continues to increase every day.

The HIPAA Enforcement Rule defines how HIPAA will be enforced and what will happen in the cases of non-compliance.[1] For even more security, the Department of Health and Human Services (HHS) also requires a number of physical and technical safeguards to minimize the risk of cyberattacks and increase the security of sensitive patient data.[2]

To make sure that entities and business associates are following HIPAA compliance, the U.S. passed a supplemental act called The Health Information Technology for Economic and

Clinical Health (HITECH) Act, which raises the penalties for any health organization that violates the HIPAA Act or any of the supporting rules.[2] While you'd think that the act and subsequent rules would clearly outline penalties that would incur, the increasing technological advances in the healthcare industry has created gray areas. More information is being used, stored, and transferred online than ever before and in an effort to keep up with these advancements, the rules need to be reinforced.

Unfortunately, it's still not enough.

Healthcare facilities like hospitals, private practices, and rehabilitation centers are at the forefront of cyberattacks. With operations becoming increasingly computerized and digital, hackers have access to more patient information than ever before. Now, physical order entry (CPOE) systems, electronic health records (EHR), and radiology, pharmacy, and laboratory systems are all becoming digital.[2] Self-service platforms allow remote access to patients, which is extremely efficient and convenient for us... until something happens. All of this efficiency and mobility comes at a price. Our risk for data breaches is higher than ever and we need to do more than simply follow HIPAA compliance rules. We need stronger security measures.

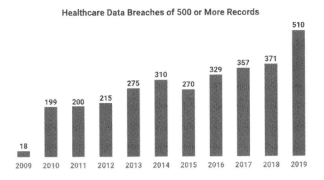

Healthcare Data Breaches of 500 or More Records

Mercy Health is a good example of the importance of strong security measures. In June 2019 it was discovered that patient information was accessible on the server from an unspecified date in 2014 to March 25, 2019.[21] For close to five full years, patient information could have been accessed by thousands of unauthorized individuals. After undergoing an audit and sweep of the breach, it was found that the protected health information of 978 patients was exposed.[21]

In 2019 alone, there were over 38 million healthcare records exposed in breaches throughout the United States.[4] When exposed, this leads to lost and stolen health records. This number is more than three times as high as 2018 and more than seven times as high as subsequent years.[4] While it falls short of the undefeated record in 2015 where 78.8 million individuals had their personal information compromised[4], it's still alarming.

Some of the most notable healthcare data breaches that occurred in 2019 include the AMCA data breach, the Dominion National data breach, the Inmediata Health Group breach, and the breaches of UW Medicine and Wolverine Solutions Group. The AMCA data breach revealed that roughly 25 million patients were affected and many of the institutions involved, including Quest and LabCorp are facing numerous investigations and lawsuits.[22] Dominion National reported a nine-year hack on its servers, which potentially breached the data of 2.96 million patients and Inmediata Health Group's misconfigured database led to a personal health data breach of 1.57 million Inmediata Health Group patients.[22] The University of Washington Medicine exposed 974,000 patients' data for three weeks due to a misconfigured server and Wolverine Solutions Group estimated that about 600,000 patients had their data compromised due to a ransomware attack that left "rolling notifications" in their system.[22]

In another catastrophic cybersecurity event, Beaumont Health System had to inform thousands of patients and former patients of a data breach that exposed sensitive personal information, including confidential health details and the Social Security numbers of some.[23] The hackers had accessed accounts between May 23, 2019 and June 3, 2019 and a third partner cybersecurity firm was swiftly brought in upon learning of the breach.[23]

When cyberattacks happen with such sensitive information, it creates widespread panic. Healthcare organizations have large volumes of information on a given individual including personal characteristics, financial records, and of course, health records—all things that you entrust to a hospital or private practice. It's a breach of trust and has caused a lot of people personal and financial loss. The problem is that hackers are deliberately targeting hospitals because of the "treasure trove" of information that they store electronically.[5] And, more often than not, by the time a hospital realizes there was a breach, hundreds, even thousands, of patient information has already been leaked.

To further understand the impact of these types of attacks, we want to talk about a few major instances that have happened in recent years. LifeLabs, a Canadian laboratory testing company, had a breach that affected 15 million customers and their private information.[6] This compromised data included names, addresses, emails, login information, dates of birth, health card numbers, and, in some circumstances, even lab results.[6] The hackers held everything hostage and LifeLabs moved forward with payment to release the stolen information, which presented a major question. How can a healthcare facility be sure that the hackers fully release the information and aren't keeping it on their hard drive for later retribution? It's impossible to know. They could come back tomorrow, next week, or next year and once again, ask for ransom.[6] Since the breach, LifeLabs has taken more intensive security measures that go above and beyond HIPAA compliance rules and have offered their customers a year of free protection—dark web monitoring and identity theft insurance—in an effort to make up for the breach.

Google's 'Project Nightingale" is another notable instance that has caused recent concerns. This project is in conjunction with the country's second-largest health system in an effort to collect detailed health information on 50 million American patients.[8] When people found out about this, it, unsurprisingly, caused an outrage and has since faced public criticism. This spark was made when people realized that Ascension started to share personally identifiable information on millions of patients with Google—without notifying or asking doctors or any of the patients for consent.[8] While Project Nightingale is said to be aimed at producing better health care, it's still a breach of information sharing, and permission should have been obtained from the patients involved prior to taking any action.

In June 2016, an anonymous hacking group, Dark Overlord, hacked into Athens Orthopedic Clinic and stole the personal information of at least 200,000 patients.[10] This information included everything from social security numbers, addresses, birth dates, health insurance details and more.[10] To release the data, they asked for a ransom and when the ransom didn't come, they made some of this personal information available for sale on the dark web.[10] If you're not familiar with the dark web, think of it as an online black market. It doesn't come up in search engines and hosts an unnerving amount of criminal activity.[14] You do **not** want your information available on the dark web.

While there are a lot of cyberattacks that occur from hackers, other cyberattacks originate from human or organizational error. For instance, Keyfactor researchers discovered an internal vulnerability in their RSA keys and certificates used by lightweight IoT devices, which greatly increased their risk of cyberattacks.[7] Their unique RSA keys—which allow data decryptions and transfers—are generated from random prime numbers or factors.[7] In theory, this is a good idea. They aim to protect online traffic and reduce the access of unauthorized users. However, after creating 175 million RSA keys, Keyfactor came to the realization that 1 out of every 172 active RSA certificates was compromised due to shared prime factors.[7] This is a huge vulnerability that could easily lead to widespread hacks and cyberattacks. Luckily, Keyfactor made the discovery before hackers did and was able to correct their mistake. If they were too late, automobiles, medical implants, and other critical devices could have been compromised and resulted in life-impacting harm.[7] Again, the implications of cyberattacks on healthcare organizations is far greater than identity theft. With remote access to medical devices, it could result in death. We need better cryptography to ensure that devices are safe and protected.

In another instance, close to 145,000 rehab patients from the Bronx-Lebanon Hospital Center in New York had their protected health information exposed.[12] This is a huge cause for concern, as rehabilitation is a very private healthcare sector and can have detrimental implications for those exposed. After determining the extent of the damage, it was found that close to 4.91 million documents were made accessible to anyone on the

Internet.[12] While the rehabilitation center caught this early and re-secured the data, it is still an example of how easy it is for institutions to make private information public.

Healthcare organizations have a unique responsibility to keep patient data safe, yet in such a hyperconnected world, it takes more than the bare minimum of following HIPAA compliance. One of the scariest aspects of cyberattacks on healthcare facilities is the fact that when medical devices are hacked, hospitals rarely even realize it.[9] This creates a direct threat to the patient's safety where the ability to provide the necessary care is hindered and these implications are terrifying. In a controlled study, doctors weren't able to easily tell that pacemakers were hacked.[9] When you go to the doctor, you're supposed to feel safe, and we need stronger data protection in place to make this a reality.

Not only do cyberattacks cause personal risk to patient information, but they also severely damage the healthcare industry as a whole. Due to the sensitivity of healthcare related information, the average cost of this kind of industry breach can reach $6.5 million.[11] The cost can be felt in terms of fewer patients, lost revenue, recovery costs, and an influx of internal investigations that can leave a healthcare facility crippled.[11] Data exposure can also be detrimental for business owners, wealthy leaders, military figures, and their families as it can be used for industrial or criminal espionage.[13] When compared to banks, hospitals and clinics have essentially no defense, yet they store invaluable information.[13] When you think of what this could mean for global security, it becomes even more serious. Information security, especially medical information security, has been a low priority and that needs to change before things get out of hand.[13]

So how do all of these cyberattacks occur if HIPAA is supposed to help mitigate these risks? In most instances of data breaches, the originating source uses phishing scams that target employees.[15] Hacking and IT incidents, like phishing scams, accounted for nearly 60% of data breaches in November 2019.[15] The remaining data breaches were a result of theft, unauthorized access, or unauthorized disclosure.[15] Similarly, of these incidents, close to 60% were due to internal threats.[16] This doesn't necessarily mean that an employee had malicious intent, however, it does cover those employees that fell for the phishing scams or weren't educated on how to properly handle the information they were given.

Because of these leaks, it's important to go above and beyond HIPAA compliance rules. We need to adapt. As the LifeLabs president and CEO, Charles Brown, eloquently put regarding the rise of cyberattacks, "...it's a wakeup call for all of us. These cyber criminals are upping their game as far as their capabilities and we all need to up our game to protect our customer data."[17] So how can we accomplish this?

One way for healthcare facilities to increase their security is to consistently make sure to follow the Department of Health and Human Services safeguards. Some of these include limited facility access, control with authorized access in place, strict policies on workstation and electronic media use and access, restrictions for transferring, removing, disposing, and re-using electronic media and ePHI, unique user IDs, an emergency access procedure, automatic log-off, encryption and decryption procedures, audit reports, tracking logs, IT disaster recovery, offsite backup, and network or transmission security that ensures HIPAA compliant hosts protect against unauthorized access to any ePHI.[2] Making sure that these measures are taken every single day across every healthcare facility will help to reduce the chances of a cyberattack occurring. As we said, it's the duty of healthcare organizations to protect their patient's health information and when they fail to do so, it creates distrust in the entire system.

Healthcare professionals should also start evaluating their current cyber strategies. Test your system, see if data is vulnerable, and make changes on a consistent basis. You can't simply assume that as technology evolves, your data will stay secure. You need to evolve your safeguards *with* technology, not after. Continual diagnostic and analysis are a great way to catch problems before they fall into the wrong hands.

A few things that need improvement are how consistently information is recorded, how to maintain configuration controls, baseline IT configurations, inventory related components, risk management, identity and access management, data protection and privacy, security training for employees, incident response protocol, and contingency planning.[18] Since internal threats are so high, a great starting point would be to host regular cyberthreat simulations for employee education and development.[16] Next, define the most valuable assets so that you can prioritize your data that's most likely to disrupt the healthcare sector if information is stolen.[16] This should include patient information, member data, and any intellectual property.[16] Spend time educating yourself on current cyber-related regulations and build security systems by design, threat intelligence, and analytics capabilities.[16] By being proactive and incorporating cybersecurity into the product before it's created, you'll stay ahead of risks and won't end up thinking about security as a mere afterthought.[16] When you're ready to launch a new system or piece of technology, try to hack it. If you can get through, it's too weak. This allows you to build resilience and test your systems before they go live.[16]

Another way to boost your healthcare data protection is to use external services that focus on safeguarding sensitive information and managing any potential cybersecurity breaches.[19] Finally, you need to make sure that when it comes time to dispose of a device, you do so safely. All healthcare technology still houses information including patient's financial or protected health information, even when it's turned off. When organizations dispose of this technology in an irresponsible way, the information is available for hackers to reach. Make sure that you know which data your organization maintains and where it's stored so that your data disposal plan can be up to date and efficient.[20] Remove any corporate marks or tags and always use a certified data destruction organization.[20] To ensure your data destruction is handled properly, opt for a company like ERI. ERI guarantees the destruction of all data via on-site or off-site destruction methods while offering value-add services such as asset registration, serialization, destruction witnessing, and more. ERI adheres to all standard compliance rules and is NAID AAA certified at all 8 facilities for data destruction and even offers demilitarization services that go above and beyond the standard need.

Chapter 12: Financial Services and Data Protection: Show Me the Money or We'll Show You the Door

Data protection is an important topic to discuss, especially when it comes to keeping sensitive personal information secure. We've seen how devastating a lack of data protection is in the healthcare sector, but that's not the only industry that needs special attention. Financial services also need to prioritize taking precautionary measures that go above and beyond the bare minimum for data protection. Hospital, retail, and financial services have been among the industries most affected by data breach events over the years, but financial cyberattacks continue to rise.[8] In 2019, 62% of breached data came from some sort of financial service, though it only accounted for 6.5% of data breaches.[22] The impact of a data breach on a financial industry is catastrophic, even if they occur less frequently. In one of the largest data breaches in history, more than 885 million records that included bank account details, Social Security digits, wire transactions, and other mortgage paperwork were found publicly accessible on the server of a major U.S. financial service company—First American Corporatoin.[23]

When businesses don't do everything in their power to protect their clients, it leads to devastating consequences—as we've seen with the recent failures in data security. Unfortunately, the data protection laws that are currently in place aren't enough and will soon face hurdles to conform to federal laws. To better understand data protection in the financial industry, let's consider the current laws in place.

The Right to Financial Privacy Act (RFPA) was introduced in 1978 and establishes specific procedures for federal government authorities to follow if they are going to obtain any information from a financial institution about a customer's records.[1] The most recent amendment, in 2001, permit the federal government greater access to customer information requested for "criminal law enforcement purposes and certain intelligence activities" without customer notice.[1] The Gramm-Leach-Bliley Act (GLBA) was enacted in 1999 and focuses on ensuring that financial institutions clearly communicate how they're going to take action to protect customer data.[2] Financial institutions include any company that offers consumer financial products or services such as loans, financial or investment advice, or insurance.[3] Later, additional guidelines were added that required banks and other financial institutions to disclose how customer information was being used outside of the company.[7] The Safeguards Rule was implementing into the GLBA by the Federal Trade Commission (FTC) to make sure that financial institutions have measures in place to keep customer information secure.[4] It was last updated in 2016. Institutions that are covered by The Safeguards Rule are responsible for taking any necessary steps to ensure that all of their affiliates and service providers are safeguarding any customer information that is in their care by proxy.[4] The GLBA in its entirety is currently being reviewed and possible changes were set to be discussed in May 2020.[3]

Other data protection acts in the financial industry include the Fair Credit Reporting Act (FCRA), which promotes the accuracy, fairness, and privacy of information in the files of consumer reporting agencies such as credit bureaus and specialty agencies.[5] The Credit and Debit Card Receipt Clarification Act is an amendment to the FCRA that requires receipts to only display 5 digits of the account numbers for increased privacy.[5] The Fair and Accurate Credit Transactions Act (FACTA) protects consumers' credit-related records and has provisions that are designed to prevent and mitigate identity theft.[6] The Disposal

Rule and The Red Flags Rule work to further protect consumer reports and notifications to data breaches. The Payment Card Industry Security Standards Council (PCI SSC) works by defining a set of compliance requirements meant to safeguard credit card transactions along with personal and financial data protection from outside attacks.[2] In 2018, this was amended to include coverage for phone-based payments. The Electronic Funds Transfer Act works to safeguard the electronic transfer of funds and the Sarbanes-Oxley Act (SOX) protects the general public alongside shareholders against fraudulent financial activity.[2] The Dodd-Frank Wall Street Reform and Consumer Act states that businesses in the financial industry cannot make misleading or inaccurate statements to consumers about the way their data will be protected. This means a company must be upfront with consumers about how their data is stored and destroyed so consumers can decide whether to trust the business or not.

While there are a lot of federal laws that encompass different facets of data protection, there is no current federal law that covers a comprehensive approach to data protection. This is where we see a problem. There are holes in the system, which makes financial institutions vulnerable. To try and mitigate these holes, a few states are taking action. With the enforcement of the GDPR sweeping European countries, and the necessity of U.S. institutions to adhere to these regulations if they have European clients, a few states have taken things into their own hands.

New York's Department of Financial Services Cybersecurity Regulations went into effect to help outline requirements for developing and implementing an effective cybersecurity program for financial institutions and financial service companies so that they can be proactive in fighting cybersecurity risks.[20] It helps enforce noncompliance so cyberattacks are prevented as much as possible. Vermont's Regulation B-2018-01 amendment of the Privacy of Consumer Financial and Health Information protects consumer information by requiring financial institutions to provide notices about privacy policies and practices, prohibits the disclosure of nonpublic personal information about consumers to nonaffiliated third parties, and requires financial institutions to obtain consumer consent prior to disclosing certain information.[21]

California introduced the California Consumer Privacy Act (CCPA) that went into effect January 1, 2020. Under this act, institutions that conduct business in California will need to implement structural changes to their privacy program, which are modeled after the GDPR.[19] These changes include the consumers right to access, delete, and port personal information provided to a company—regardless of the industry—up to two times in a 12-month period, and requires that institutions establish secure processes to verify consumers' identity and authorization to access information.[19] Fines are steep and enforcement is going to be more strict than past regulations.

Data protection and privacy is important, especially for institutions in the financial sectors. The amount of sensitive information that banks and financial institutions gather, manage, and store means that any data breaches could lead to dire, life-changing consequences for consumers. Financial data protection alone was one of the driving forces that led to the extreme enforcement surrounding the GDPR and is another reason why the United States federal government has started to re-examine our regulations. The EU ultimately felt that there needed to be more consequences for any business that failed to keep such sensitive information safeguarded.[7] As we discussed in Chapter 5, the GDPR made it necessary to obtain clear and understood consent, made any data collected on individuals anonymous to make identification more difficult, required industries to notify clients of data breaches immediately, and even appointed enforcement officers to ensure that these policies were being carried out.[7]

Now consider how your financial information is processed and secured at a bank or related organization. You divulge your social security number, credit card information, lending history, account numbers, address, name, date of birth, and more. Then, workers use this information to verify accounts, withdrawals, and hundreds of other transactions ranging from in-person, over the phone, or online. When employees or officials working at financial institutions fail to adequately protect this data or use lenient security protocols, your data becomes vulnerable to hackers or breaches related to employee error. Divulging this type of sensitive personal information has become so common during business transactions in the digital age and the occurrence of data breach threats continues to rise, so what we're doing in the U.S. obviously isn't working.

While the EU's GDPR applies to businesses in the U.S. that have clients living in any country in the European Union, we don't have current legislation to protect American citizens. It has spurred similar efforts, as we discussed in Chapter 6, but as of April 2020, we have yet to see federal legislation passed. There's also been pushback from institutions like Microsoft and Amazon, who rely on selling customer data as a source of revenue.[7] Instead, what we have now is a patchwork of different types of legislation that's implemented on an industry-specific basis. We've seen a few changes regarding state laws, such as those discussed previously in this chapter from California and Vermont but having state-by-state laws could end up causing difficulty for industries that work on a national level. It's complicated and creates the opportunity for more cracks to appear in data protection. As of March 2018, all 50 U.S. states have implemented some sort of data privacy regulations in addition to the District of Columbia, Guam, Puerto Rico, and the U.S. Virgin Islands.[7] The problem is that these laws vary in what they regulate and don't cover data protection in full. Some states are very restrictive while others only added regulations requiring customer notification in the instance of a data breach.

In the past, being compliant with the laws was all a financial company had to worry about. However, we've seen that this is no longer enough. As hackers continue to develop increasingly sophisticated attack methods, it's been made obvious that data security needs to be an ongoing and more complex task.[7] We also need to clarify the issues that are currently happening with consent in the digital age. A lot of people don't realize what they're signing away when they agree to terms of service because institutions elongate these terms and use misleading language or terms that are difficult for non-financial experts to understand. With the hundreds of data breaches that have been occurring and the millions of people being affected, we need to do more than the bare minimum. Financial industries continue to be a primary target and are going to continue to stay in the spotlight until information is made more secure.

The number of financial data breaches and document leaks that have occurred over the past few years is uncomfortable to think about. In 2019, more than 24 million financial and banking documents were found online when a server's security lapsed.[10] The server was running an Elasticsearch database and had over a decade's worth of highly sensitive financial and tax data that represented tens of thousands of loans and mortgages from some of the largest banks in the United States.[10] They included CitiFinancial, a now-defunct arm of Citigroup, files from HSBC Life Insurance, Wells Fargo, CapitalOne, and even a few U.S. federal departments.[10] The sensitive information included names, addresses, social security numbers, bank account numbers, checking account information, and even tax documents like W-2s. For roughly two weeks, none of this information was protected with a password so virtually anyone could access and read the documents.[10] Thankfully, the leak was found by an independent security researcher and the database was shut down before hackers were able to do anything with the information, but this never should have happened in the first place. After looking into the leak, it was found to be traced back to Ascension, a data and analytics company for the financial industry.[10] As of now, there was no punitive action taken as a result of this leak.

In July 2019, Capital One reported a massive data breach that affected 100 million people in the United States.[14] Of this, approximately 140,000 credit card customers had their social security numbers stolen and another 80,000 had their bank account numbers exposed.[14] This happened due to a firewall vulnerability that was taken advantage of by a 33-year-old Seattle woman named Paige Thompson.[14] Due to diligence, Paige was arrested and Capital One has patched the problem, but it still shows the ease of accessibility when there are problems in security.

Wells Fargo also has a history of alarming financial problems. In 2016, it was revealed that Wells Fargo was opening accounts and new credit cards in its customers' names without telling them or gaining consent.[13] Since then they've failed to maintain adequate risk management and compliance practices and continued to sell unnecessary products.[13] As a result, former president Trump and federal regulatory offices imposed a $1 billion fine on Wells Fargo.[13]

One of the most well-known data breaches in the financial industry is the Equifax data breach of 2017. This is arguably one of the biggest catalysts for changing the current financial regulatory guidelines and expectations. Back in September 2017, Equifax, a credit bureau dealing with millions of individuals' financial information, was breached. This breach compromised sensitive personal information of over 145 million individuals.[11] The information included social security numbers, driver's license numbers, dates of birth, credit and debit card numbers, and the subsequent names of corresponding individuals.[12] Not only was this information breached, but it was also stolen by hackers. The main reason this Equifax data breach was so bad was because it was due to the direct actions of Equifax and its failure to act—it violated both the FTC Act and the Gramm-Leach-Bliley Safeguards Rule.[12] Equifax failed to check employee action during sensitive processes, failed to detect a patch required due to automated processes, and failed to segment the network.[12] Due to the lack of segmenting, once the hackers gained access to one database, they were able to access any part of the network they wanted to without any extra work. This meant even more sensitive information in addition to administrative credentials. This breach was entirely preventable. Had Equifax adhered to the federal guidelines and simple security updates, it could have reduced the impact of this breach ten-fold. Even if hackers would have gained access, the devastating results and amount of breached information could have been severely diminished. However, Equifax failed to update security certifications that had expired 10 months earlier and therefore didn't notice the breach for over four months.[12] By the time it was noticed, it was too late. As of today, this is considered one of the most severe exposures of Americans' personal data that's ever happened.[11] As a result, Equifax was required to pay around $650 million to settle federal and state investigations with consumer claims that referred to the data breach.[11] Since then, Equifax has also spent hundreds of millions of dollars to improve its technology and subsequent security systems.[11]

In the wake of the disastrous data breaches that we've seen, there are three emerging trends regarding data privacy. These trends include the evolution of data breaches, regulatory evolution and advancements, and technological adoption.[9] There are increasing threats of data breaches due to the increase in severity of malware programs, the growing number of malicious "insiders" who put the institution at risk, and a number of unintentional user mistakes.[9] We also see data breaches becoming more common due to improper hardware destruction or people reselling hardware without completely wiping the data first. We're seeing more of a push towards harmonizing data protection standards across the nation, especially as states are starting to take things into their own hands. This has put more pressure on the federal government to conform to an overarching regulatory legislation. However, we've also seen an advancement in technology and with that, more technological adoptions for goods and services.

To better understand this, consider the implications of artificial intelligence in financial institutions. Advancements in technology make it easier and faster to collect, store, and analyze sensitive personal information. We're using more smart devices to help make our daily lives convenient and even healthier, but a lot of people don't realize that when you have to use a credit card with these devices, you're giving the institutions access to sensitive financial information alongside behavioral information. Algorithms can analyze your every movement and relay them back to institutions that could affect financial premiums, insurance rates, or benefits. In 2018, the life insurance company

John Hancock began to offer customers the option to wear a fitness tracker.[15] If you were healthy and active, your premiums would go down. While this is extremely cutting edge, it raises a lot of questions around data protection and industries tied to finances. Not only will it put more of your sensitive information at risk, but a lot of people also worry that it will lead to discrimination and unfair algorithms. It's an interesting thing to consider as technological advancements continue to develop alongside data protection laws.

All things considered, on March 5, 2019 the Federal Trade Commission (FTC) announced a proposal to the GLBA Safeguards Rule that would expand the scope of institutions covered by the rule and mandate that covered entities take clearly defined steps to secure customer information.[16] It represented a major shift to a more top-down approach and hopefully will lead to more institutional compliance with encryption and multifactor authentication rules. The goal is to design more secure, confidential processes for storing, managing, and analyzing customer information. In creating clear-cut guidelines, we hope there will be stronger enforcement measures to ensure financial institutes are working in line with their customers' best interests. The proposed requirements of the expanded Safeguards Rule include developing a cybersecurity incident response plan, periodically performing risk assessments to stay up-to-date on security programs and ahead of security breaches, restricting access, encrypting all customer information, regardless of where it's at, using audit trails, developing procedures for the secure disposal of customer information, monitoring and detecting unauthorized users, implementing ongoing training procedures, and more.[16] These expansions are supposed to go into effect at some point in 2021. It's a great step in the right direction for financial institutions' increased data protection.

Unfortunately, it's still not enough. Currently, around half of Americans believe that their personal information is *less* secure than it was five years ago.[17] The United States still operates under a patchwork of these sector-specific laws that fail to adequately protect citizens and even the laws in place suffer from complicated or lenient enforcement policies. Making a switch to something similar to the GDPR would be far less complicated and would result in more compliant financial industries. It would also strengthen and bring the U.S. in line with the emerging data-protection norms around the world.[17] While a few states have taken things into their own hands, as we discussed previously in this chapter, we need a stronger cohesive plan.

To help further mitigate data breaches, financial institutions should go above and beyond the current laws and regulations in place. We need to move our focus to implementing smart policies from the start, which includes making sure that employees are trained and educated on what to do with this sensitive information. Some suggestions include not opening or responding to any suspicious emails, making sure that websites are secure and contain no openings for hackers, keeping up security firewalls and only using secure networks when transporting data, securing data within the organization, monitoring personal devices used by employees when accessing company systems, encrypting data sent over public networks, restricting access of certain data to select employees with security clearance, and performing periodic audits of security practices to catch any loopholes and keep everything up-to-date.[7] A comprehensive data protection program that capitalizes on privacy should be prioritized across the board. For financial industries to take added precautions, they should consider centrally managing endpoint solutions, aligning global security with real-time threat alerts, proactively protecting data through individual systems, servers, networks, and endpoints, implementing automated compliance controls, and integrating security solutions with regular operations.[18] It's also important for financial institutions to make sure that they're handling hardware data destruction responsibly.

Even before the GDPR and specific industry related data protection regulations were in place, ERI has been here to help destroy sensitive personal information to the highest standard— 100% destruction. Institutions that were smart knew that the laws set in place weren't enough and they needed to go above and beyond the standards to make sure things were taken care of properly. ERI is here to help you achieve this by ensuring that old or outdated electronics don't pose a risk to your company. For added security measures, we offer both on-site and off-site destruction. To strengthen the importance of responsible data destruction, keep in mind that to comply with the GLBA, financial businesses must ensure data is being destroyed so that it cannot be read or reconstructed.

Chapter 13: Retailers and Data Protection: Protecting Your Clients' Data

While the financial industry is the industry that incurs the highest costs after a breach, they are not affected by breaches nearly as often as retailers. According to the 2018 Thales Data Threat Report, Retail Edition, United States retailers lead the world in security breaches. From 2017 to 2018, retail breaches have more than doubled, rising from 19% to 50%.[1] The increase in breaches is alarming, to say the least, but what's even more eye-opening is when the data from U.S. breaches is compared to global retail breaches. Global retail breaches averaged about 27% in 2018, almost half of what the United States reported.[1] The total number of U.S. retailers that have reported at data breach at any time during their operation in the past is up to about 75%, with close to half of those occurring from 2017-2018.[1] Retail data breaches have been rising all over the country and now comprise the second most breached segment in the U.S., trailing only slightly behind the U.S. federal government and ranking slightly ahead of healthcare and financial services.[1] A lot of this increase comes from the realization that many retailers haven't taken IT security seriously and have failed to enforce preventative measures. However, due to the recent influx of data breaches, U.S. retailers are planning to significantly increase their IT security spending and preventative security measures.

In a data breach involving the popular rideshare company Uber Technologies Inc, hackers stole the personal data of 57 million customers and drivers.[2] The information included names, email addresses, and phone numbers of 50 million riders and affected another 7 million drivers.[2] Of the 7 million drivers affected, roughly 600,000 had their driver's license numbers compromised.[2] While Uber has reported that there have been no evidence of fraudulent activity tied to this breach, it's not something that the public has been happy about—and for good reason. In subsequent efforts to try to downplay the severity of this attack, Uber concealed this data breach for more than a year. To help with this effort, Uber paid the hackers $100,000 for their discretion and promise to delete the data.[2] When this became public knowledge, many customers and drivers were shocked to hear that Uber kept such a massive data breach secret for over a year. This led to criticism from many people regarding how the breach was handled and thousands of riders and drivers vowed to stop working with Uber. To try and mitigate damages, Uber has offered free credit protection monitoring and identity theft protection to all drivers who had their driver's license information compromised. Unfortunately, this isn't the first time that Uber has flouted regulations. Hopefully, the new CEO will make the necessary changes to uphold current data protection laws and ensure swift notification when breaches occur.

Before discussing another retail data breach, it's important to consider a few things that the Uber data breach has taught us. First, institutions need to realize that covering up a data breach is often far worse than the data breach itself. Not only do you increase personal risk, but you're also ruining your reputation and consumer-trust. Another thing that we need to stress is that institutions should *never* reward hackers, no matter what the circumstances are. By rewarding hackers, all you're doing is sending a message to other criminals that crime does pay, which simply creates incentive to do it again. You make yourself vulnerable and directly communicate that you negotiate with criminals. Yet about 66% of retailers and wholesalers that were surveyed admitted to paying ransom to a hacker at some point between 2017 and 2018.[4] The ideal course of action after a data breach involves notifying the appropriate authorities and working with them to help reduce the consequences of the breach. You need to be honest and comply with all regulations in place if you want to avoid hefty fines, customer backlash, and an excessive number of lawsuits.

In May of 2019, Checker's Restaurant, one of the largest drive-through restaurants in the U.S., was attacked through Point of Sale (POS) malware.[10] This attack impacted 15% of their stores across the U.S. and the sensitive information of an identifiable number of customers. This data included cardholder names, credit card numbers, verification codes, and expiration dates.[10] These third-party attacks are growing in prevalence and demonstrates that better security measures need to be taken. With the average third-party data breach costing $7.5 million to remediate, it's important for retailers to start taking a stronger risk-based approach.[10] Similar third-party attacks happened to Hy-Vee in August 2019.[10]

In 2017, after another large-scale incident, Forever 21 data was breached for at least seven months.[10] The hack was reported in January of 2018, but the compromised POS devices throughout the duration of the breach gave hackers unique access to customers' payment cards and personal information.[10]

Adidas faced a breach in June 2018. The company became aware of an unauthorized party that claimed to have acquired millions of customer contact information, usernames, and encrypted passwords.[4] They didn't believe that the breach included any credit card information or fitness data, but it could have used encrypted passwords to gain access to this information later on.[4] The main difference between Adidas and the previous accounts was that Adidas disclosed the breach almost immediately to make sure and avoid weakening their consumers' trust and confidence.[4] This happened only a few months after MyFitnessPal was hacked and 150 million accounts were compromised.[4] The target on sports and fitness retailers has grown since these apps and websites have started to collect more personal data on their activity. Additionally, the overall growth of e-commerce and mobile payment methods has led to an increase in opportunities for hackers to infiltrate retail databases and steal customer information.[4]

In September 2019 DoorDash announced that a breach occurred on May 4, 2018 that affected any user who had created an account prior to April 5, 2018.[11] This breach affected 4.9 million customers, delivery workers, and merchants who had information stolen by hackers including names, email and delivery addresses, order history, phone numbers, and passwords.[11] The problem is that when data is breached, even if it doesn't include credit card information or financial details, consumers are still at risk for identity theft or fraud for many years. It's often difficult to track individual problems with data breaches because they can occur years after the initial breach. Instead, institutions need to see these lawsuits as warning signs to take stronger preventive measures and to boost their cybersecurity efforts.

In 2019, WaWa, a popular convenience store along the East coast, had POS malware planted in the systems of over 850 locations that went undetected for eight months.[11] This malware harvested the payment information from a number of customers including their names, card numbers, and the associated expiration dates. Earl Enterprise restaurants that include Planet Hollywood, Buca di Beppo, and Earl of Sandwich faced a similar POS malware problem. Between May 2018 and March

2019, two million customer credit cards were stolen from over 100 restaurants belonging to this enterprise.[11]

Another incident that reached public attention was when Macy's incurred a second data breach of their customers' information within a two-year time span. The most recent one occurred in October 2019 and affected countless numbers of credit cards.[6] The team at Macy's has been hesitant to release numbers, but the information that was affected included customer names, addresses, phone numbers, credit card numbers, card verification codes, and expiration dates—all of which greatly increase the chances of fraudulent activity and identity theft.[6] This comes after the 2018 breach where credit card data and passwords were stolen from 0.5% of Macy's customer base—which translates to millions of people's information.[6] Both breaches have changed the way people view Macy's security procedures; they're now often seen as careless, lazy, reckless, and even negligent.

One of the most discussed retail data breaches has been the breach involving Marriott International. This is one of the largest known breaches of personal data to date—even larger than Equifax's 2017 security incident.[7] On November 30, 2018, Marriott announced a data breach that affected about 500 million people.[7] In a statement, it was disclosed that since 2014, criminal hackers had unfettered access to a database that had stored the personal information for millions of guests staying in hotels operated by Starwood, a Marriott subsidiary.[7] As a response, Marriott has faced lawsuits from a number of different states and individuals. This isn't the first time a hotel has been a huge target. Hotels and other retail industries have been known for lax security measures that need to be changed going forward. Also involved was Accenture, the consulting firm handling all of the technology for Starwood. In addition to suing Marriott

International, many people are turning to Accenture and blaming them for a failure to prevent these types of security problems.[8] With the new passage of state laws like the California Consumer Privacy Act, we're hoping to see a decrease in these occurrences in the future.

In the meantime, retailers need to start considering their security measures and do more than simple recommendations to mitigate data breaches. One way to do this is through responsibly handling point-of-sale (POS) equipment. The devices that are commonly used for retail sales often include printers for contracts, applications for store credit cards, smartphones or tablets with plug-in card readers for credit and debit card transactions, and computer or cash register terminals for POS information. All of these devices are capable of storing details like credit card numbers, names, addresses, contact information, social security numbers, and more. This is not only a vulnerability for hackers, but it can also be detrimental if improperly recycled. When retailers upgrade their POS electronics, a lot of them don't realize that you need to recycle outdated equipment in a very secure manner. If you're just bringing it to any recycling center without asking questions and verifying their recycling process, you're making a mistake. POS systems should be recycled in a way that securely destroys the data 100% to eliminate any risk of hackers accessing the hardware. Point-of-sale data breaches, alongside website outages, are some of the most threatening types of data breaches in terms of potential severity.[9]

Retailers are finally beginning to understand the severity of the risk that they face with data breaches. The increase in recognition is good news and means that more retailers are realizing the importance of preventative measures. While 84% are planning on increasing their IT budgets to help mitigate data breaches, a lot of experts don't think that this is going to be effective.[1] The problem is that they're wasting their money on the wrong preventative practices. Many of the affected retailers are investing in defenses, but they need to allocate their money towards effective defense plans appropriately. Since roughly three-quarters of data breaches in the retail industry tend to be inside jobs—either intentionally or accidentally—there needs to be a higher focus on employee training. Teaching employees how to handle sensitive data is one way to avoid accidental breaches and it's important to use strong passwords for any point-of-sale system. Consequences for violation need to be communicated, emphasized regularly, and appropriately enforced. Another way to reduce the severity of retail data breaches is to put a plan in place to get notifications if breaches occur and how to stop the breach in its tracks.

A less invasive, straightforward way to reduce the number of retail data breaches is to make sure that retailers conduct due diligence prior to working with third party vendors. The amount of data breaches involving third parties continues to rise, but it's preventable when proper action is taken. Retailers should always understand how a third-party will protect any sensitive data that is accessed, processed, and shared with them. They also need to know how long the third-party will keep this data and how it will be destroyed when it's no longer needed. Lastly, they need a well-established, third-party risk management process to ensure regular security checks are performed on these vendors. When it comes to data destruction, ERI will make sure that your sensitive data is safe. We're the largest recycler of electronic waste in the world with facilities all across the United States and have certified partners in over 140 countries all across the world.

Every retailer has different needs, but all electronics eventually need to be recycled. Regardless of if you use electronics in your store or sell electronics to consumers, making sure that the electronics are handled responsibly is one of the best ways to reduce the threat of data breaches. To further enhance data protection, retailers should always responsibly recycle their point-of-sale (POS) equipment with a trusted company like ERI. We offer a number of different on-site pick up programs along with options to mail-in your old POS systems. From here, we'll make sure that the data is completely destroyed prior to recycling the electronics.

While there have been a lot of data breaches in the retail sector, it's important to note that retailers were some of the first businesses to step forward and say, "Hey, we don't care that states are passing e-waste bans or don't have legislation in place for proper disposal, we want to do the right thing." Since 2006, we've seen a rise in retailers contacting us to create responsible e-waste pick up sites. BestBuy contacted us in 2006 and said that they were interested in giving up a portion of their retail space in order to provide a box for consumers to come and safely return all electronics for recycling. Unfortunately, there was a lot of pushback from other institutions. Other retailers were saying that it would be a disaster and that you can't use retail space for e-waste recycling or organized drop-offs. Best Buy persevered and decided to work with ERI to test pilot 10 stores for electronic waste recycling. Shortly after, it moved to 20 stores, then 50 stores. Now, every Best Buy in America offers safe electronic waste recycling drop offs in collaboration with ERI. Millions and millions of people use this service every year to drop off their electronic waste at Best Buy, who is currently working towards a goal of recycling two billion pounds of electronic waste.

This was just the beginning. Many other retailers have since followed suit and enacted take back programs with ERI. Staples and Costco are two other retailers that work with ERI in a large capacity. We also have partnerships with Target, Walmart, Amazon, and more. Originally, they all wanted to do the environmentally friendly thing, especially as more and more people took a green initiative. However, with the recent focus on data protection and the importance of proper data destruction, these organizations are now committed to making sure they protect their corporate assets *and* their constituent's information. They started for environmental and sustainable reasons—all of which remain valid and active, but soon morphed to include the realization that their customers needed a better way to have their data destroyed as well.

To make sure that you're doing everything you can as a retailer, you need to properly handle your old POS equipment and any other electronics that you use in your business. However, remember that not all recyclers work the same. You need to make sure that data destruction is done properly so that it's impossible for anyone to access hard drives and steal sensitive information. Typically, this is done through one of three methods: wiping, degaussing, or shredding. Wiping uses specific software to delete all of the information on a drive. When it's not done correctly, the information is still salvageable. Degaussing uses magnetic fields to demagnetize drives, which eliminates all data and destroys the hard drive completely. After degaussing, the hard drive cannot be used. This is the preferred method of the NSA. Finally, shredding involves putting the hard drive or POS system through a giant shredder that grinds the device into small pieces. Shredding ensures that 100% of the data is physically destroyed. Once your POS system or electronics are destroyed, they can be broken down into raw commodities for recycling and utilized for beneficial reuse. ERI offers these methods of recycling done with precision every time and ensures 100% data destruction.

Chapter 14: Military and Data Protection: Homeland Insecurity Comes to the U.S.

The healthcare, financial, and retail industries aren't the only ones affected by problems with cybersecurity. In an alarming realization, the United States' military is also failing at protecting Americans from national data breaches. While there are a number of statutes in place to protect U.S. citizens, the government isn't following the data protection measures very well. The Federal Information Security Management Act was established in 2002 and sets information security standards for federal agencies to follow. In turn, federal agencies are required to comply by reporting any security problems or data breaches when they occur so that the Department of Homeland Security can step in and help. In 2014, the act was amended and became the Federal Information Security Modernization Act. While the name changed, the underlying rules are the same. Federal agencies are required to keep people's information private and need to notify Congress immediately if or when a breach occurs.

Each year the Office of the Inspector General audits government agencies to make sure they're complying with the Federal Information Security Modernization Act. During this audit, many different agencies receive ratings that are deemed "not effective." Weaknesses are found in data protection and privacy, risk management, configurations, incident responses, monitoring and planning. The agencies that were found to have problems couldn't detect/identify, protect, respond, or recover. For example, one thing that was discovered was that the Department of Health and Human Services had no way to identify the software that was installed on their systems. If an external software was installed, either by an employee or another malicious actor, it would go unnoticed indefinitely. To fix these problems, the Government Accountability Office made plenty of recommendations. However, the frightening reality was that the agency never took any steps to correct the problems, despite the recommendations.

The Department of Defense is another agency that is absolutely terrible at their cybersecurity efforts. In an audit conducted by the Inspector General in September 2018, 266 open cybersecurity-related problems were found that dated back to 2008.[4] All of these problems received recommendations on how to fix them, but they continued to remain untouched. The cybersecurity vulnerabilities are a solemn threat to national security and need to be taken more seriously across the board. In a similar instance, the Inspector General had recommended that the Pentagon takes 159 different steps to improve security.[4] In the end, the Pentagon only took 19 of them. Doors to server sites are casually left unlocked, officials use very weak and vulnerable passwords, and offices don't encrypt data when transferring from computers via USB sticks and removable drives.[4] In fact, less than 1% of Controlled Unclassified Information stored on removable media was found to be encrypted at the Department of Defense.[4] Keep in mind that these are the people responsible for protecting our country from foreign attacks. Not only would a data breach be expensive, but it would also be dangerous to American citizens and Homeland Security.

The U.S. Missile Defense Agency also has a number of cybersecurity vulnerabilities. An October report from the Government Accountability Office pointed out a number of fatal flaws in the Pentagon's weapon's systems that made them particularly vulnerable to cyberattacks.[4] One thing to keep in mind is these cybersecurity problems aren't just dangerous because they involve missile defense systems and control over new weapons—it also leaves millions of soldiers at risk for personal attacks.[4] Patient medical records can be easily accessed if the server isn't secure enough, but it doesn't seem like anyone is enforcing the standards needed to keep this information safe. Without the proper governance, cybersecurity risks will continue to go unnoticed and may lead to malicious actors gaining access to disrupt or destroy our informational systems.

Unfortunately, it's already become a problem. Software hacks are on the rise and are only getting more attention. In 2017, the Internal Revenue Service (IRS) announced that its Data Retrieval Tool used by college students in need of financial aid was breached. Over 100,000 students were compromised during his breach. The Securities and Exchange Commission (SEC) database was also breached in 2019. In this breach, countless records containing corporate and financial data were stolen, and many people believed that this information could easily be taken advantage of by stock traders. In 2017, data that was stored on the U.S. Army Intelligence and Security Command (INSCOM) was breached. INSCOM is home to incredibly sensitive information, including software that is used for classified communication. Other agencies that have been targeted in the past include the United States Navy, Election Assistance Commission, the Department of Defense, the Department of Energy, and more.

In 2015, there was a breach of the Office of Personnel Management, where hackers stole files on an estimated 21.5 million people who had applied for government jobs.[5] The U.S. government believes that the hackers were related to Chinese Intelligence groups. During the breach, they gained access to social security numbers of these 21.5 million people—which equated to roughly 1 in every 15 Americans at the time.[5] After doing some investigative research, the Office of Personnel Management stated that they believe anyone who applied for background check from 2000 on was likely to have had their information compromised.[5]

In October 2018, the Pentagon revealed a cyber breach of the Department of Defense's travel records.[6] This breach compromised the personal information and credit card data of roughly 30,000 U.S. military and civilian personnel.[6] A report conducted in 2020 estimates that the U.S. government and military experienced roughly 83 data breaches in 2019, which accounted for 5.6% of the year's total breaches and resulted in the exposure of 3.6 million sensitive records.[7]

Most recently, the U.S. Defense Information System Agency (DISA) announced that it experienced a substantial data breach. In February 2020, this information was released to the public. DISA is an arm of the U.S. Department of Defense that handles secure communications and IT for the president and others.[7] DISA is also responsible for overseeing the president's secure calls, establishing support communication networks in combat zones, and taking care of military cybersecurity issues.[9] The breach was said to affect about 200,000 people, but there has not been any indication that the data breached has been misused.[8] The breach was discovered through a security check and has since been fixed, but there is a lack of transparency occurring and many victims have no idea what the scope of the breach really was.[8] All that we know is that DISA sent a letter to those affected saying that names and social security numbers may have been compromised and that the victims would receive free credit monitoring.[7] The details surrounding this cybersecurity breach remain unknown.

We need to keep in mind that for a full-spectrum approach to cybersecurity, we have to include hardware protection. Hardware is still vulnerable, as made evident by the

Veteran's Administration Case. The Veteran's Administration Case was one of the largest data breaches to date that was related to hardware. In 2006, an employee of the Veteran's Administration took a laptop and an external hard drive home, and it was subsequently stolen. On these devices, there were over 26 million military and veteran records. The VA had to then pay $20 million to the people affected by the breach. While there are a lot of questions about why the employee took the information home to begin with, it still shows the vulnerabilities that unmonitored hardware carries. This includes hardware that is no longer in use or needed.

Over the course of this book, we've continued to stress the problem that we're facing with e-waste. The Environmental Protection Agency (EPA) estimates that only about 12.5% of electronic waste is recycled and the rest ends up in a landfill somewhere across the country. While e-waste only accounts for about 2% of all of the trash in landfills, it makes up 70% of the total toxic trash. Once in landfills, chemicals seek into the ground and contaminate air and water. Yet, as we've stressed, recycling e-waste responsibly doesn't just keep the environment safe—it keeps our data safe. Unfortunately, even U.S. national security departments fail to do this. With all of the sophisticated equipment men and women in the military need to perform their jobs and keep them safe, you'd think that Homeland Security would start to take e-waste seriously. If any of the equipment used in the military malfunctions or is hacked, the results would be detrimental to our troops and citizens. Unfortunately, the armed forces often purchase counterfeit or at-risk electronics and don't have a formalized way to dispose of their electronic waste.

After an investigation in 2009 and 2010, it was uncovered that 1,800 cases of counterfeit electronic parts were being used in the national defense system. Close to 70% of these electronic parts originated in China and while they were discovered and removed from use, things could have gone a completely different direction. This was a problem regarding manufacturing and buying technology that wasn't secure, but unfortunately, it's not the only time it's happened. Despite numerous warnings of cybersecurity threats, the U.S. Department of Defense (DoD) has continued to purchase electronics known to have security vulnerabilities. In 2018, the DoD bought electronics worth over $32.8 million with known security vulnerabilities.[1] Included in these electronics were Lexmark devices, which is a China-based company. In the past, Lexmark has been linked to the Chinese military and the country's nuclear and cyberespionage program.[1] The DoD also had purchased Lenovo computers. They were originally banned in 2016 from being used with the State Department's classified networks after numerous reports that Lenovo computers were manufactured with hidden hardware and software commonly used for cyberespionage.[1] Despite this ban and the obvious threat that it provides, the Army bought 195 Lenovo products in 2018 and the Air Force purchased another 1,378 Lenovo products.[1]

Purchasing hardware that is a known threat completely offsets measures that are taken to protect national security. While the U.S. has devoted billions of dollars to securing critical infrastructures and defense systems, they've focused almost entirely on software.[2] A change needs to be made and soon, otherwise we're going to see the detrimental effects that come from hacked hardware. An easy way to increase the focus on hardware data protection involves creating a formalized way to dispose of electronic waste. As of now, nothing exists. Many military channels irresponsibly recycle their old electronics by using uncertified e-waste recyclers. When this happens, their e-waste is shipped to countries overseas such as Thailand, India, Pakistan, China, the Middle East, and other developing nations.

Once it gets to these countries, the e-waste is sorted by hand, parts shipped to facilities, and then certain components are processed to make them look new again. Instead of recycling them, these countries simply sand down electronic components to "remove" identifying information. If the hardware wasn't properly wiped, the information will still be accessible on the "new" devices that are being created from old parts. What's worse is that these electronic devices are often sold back to the military or private buyers. Not only does this decrease reliability, but it also creates a huge risk for cybersecurity in the military.

Other military channels are taking action that many people see as even worse. In early 2019, the Navy commissioned incineration facilities to burn nearly 2 tons of electronic storage devices. Researchers at the Naval Surface Warfare Center stored classified information on these digital devices and wanted to destroy them by the most secure and irreversible means.[3] What they didn't realize is that burning these devices wasn't the best way to do this. Unfortunately, they went forward and burned about 4,000 pounds of IT equipment including magnetic, optical and solid-state storage devices—all of which contained sensitive, classified data.[3] They believed this was the best way to ensure that the electronic devices were destroyed without incident. Yet responsible recycling companies like ERI could have offered a much better solution. Burning electronic waste releases thousands of toxic chemicals into the air, which has detrimental effects on the health of those in surrounding areas.

ERI has earned both e-Stewards certification and R2 Standards certification, which means that we account for the final destination of all e-waste in our facilities and have proven that we process all electronic waste locally rather than shipping it overseas. So, we contribute to reducing the number of counterfeit parts and data breaches from hardware. We also offer

a demilitarized data destruction service, which specifically
covers data destruction of top-secret materials. Only essential
personnel are allowed in the area where the data destruction
takes place and only demilitarized recycling projects occur in
that specific area. All of the materials go to the facility under the
watchful eye of the client contractor and a government
representative—both of whom will sign that they witnessed the
destruction.

ERI carries the National Association of Information
Destruction (NAID) AAA certification, which means that we're
committed to protecting sensitive data through every step of the
e-waste recycling process. We provide the option for our clients
to watch a live video feed of their data being destroyed and
provide certificates of destruction. Finally, we have a data breach
response plan in place—just in case. While data breaches are
rare in certified vendors who take intricate security precautions,
it's still important to be prepared. ERI allows for the secure
destruction of government agencies' electronic waste and has a
tested system in place to ensure that sensitive and confidential
information is tracked from the moment it's acquired until it's
been destroyed. We also recommend establishing a plan for
transporting retired IT assets from your facility to the vendor's
facility. This may or may not include having a federal employee
transit alongside the electronic waste for security purposes.
Making sure that you're prepared, avoiding the purchase of at-
risk electronics, responsibly recycling your e-waste, and
destroying the data contained on your devices are the best ways
to reduce military data breaches and protect national security.

Chapter 15: The Auto Industry and Data Protection: Back to the Future or Square One?

As technology continues to advance across all industries and the Internet of Things becomes more prevalent in our daily lives, we've seen a sharp increase in the trend of smart cars. Over the past decade, automobiles have transformed into elaborate machines. Automobiles today store private information about our personal lives, such as GPS data about our homes and offices, the routes we take and when we take them, the names of our family members, phone numbers, all of the data that's on our cellular devices, and more. Plus, the implications of hacking into one device have a cascading chain effect that many of us have difficulty wrapping our heads around. If someone hacks into your automobile and it's connected to your phone, they can then access the data on your phone, computer, tablet, wearable devices, or any other smart technology. Hacking into one of our devices bridges every aspect of our life, especially as we become even more interconnected.

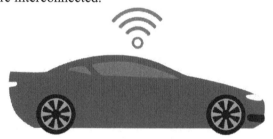

In the past, even with minor technological advancements, automobiles were never considered to be a hacking opportunity. It simply wasn't worth the effort. Now, a majority of people are driving around in vehicles that have millions of lines of computer code and convenient connectivity options. You pair your phone, iPod, or headset to your car without thinking because these features are fairly futuristic and allow you to enhance your driving time. When we're asked about these advancements and how they're related to cybersecurity, it's a pretty straightforward answer. The bottom line is that automobiles have become computers on wheels, which means that they're now at a higher risk for cyberattacks. In fact, your car is a lot easier to hack than you might think. This becomes even more true when we look at the shift toward autonomous driving, which relies on sensors, cameras, and radar use.[3] It's estimated that 25% of automobiles on the road in 2030 will be autonomous or self-driving.[1] In addition, it's estimated that by 2023, some 775 million automobiles will be connected to the Internet in some way—up 330 million in 2018.[3] More technology leads to more potential problems and they need to be addressed.

The more new, sophisticated features are added to our everyday automobiles, the more vulnerable we are to cyberattacks—it's as simple as that. Added features require hundreds of thousands of lines of computer code working behind the scenes to ensure proper functionality and to avoid malfunctions. As of 2018, it was found that the average car has over 150 million lines of computer code and some have even more than a Boeing 787.[3] There are German automobiles with 330-gigabyte hard drives—five times as much as an iPhone 11.[8] Pair this with the thousands of pieces of hardware that are put together to give you your favorite features and it becomes a problem. Advanced technology with millions of lines of computer code creates a complexity that becomes difficult to safeguard, especially when manufacturers aren't considering cybersecurity issues during software design. The sad truth is that until recently, the automotive industry vastly underestimated the implications of a hack into smart car technology. With millions of lines of computer code, there are millions of ways for hackers to gain access to a vehicle. Every year, as automobiles continue to advance, these threats become more serious. Software vulnerabilities are more accessible to malicious actors now that we have cellular networks, Wi-Fi, and physical connections to exploit any miniscule vulnerability and this fact often goes overlooked.[1]

To combat these cybersecurity vulnerabilities, European privacy regulators are setting new rules for how connected automobiles process and share consumers' personal data with software providers, insurance firms, and other institutions.[11] These regulators understand the risks of vulnerable hacks into automobiles and want to ensure that they're doing whatever they can to limit them and reduce the potential for malicious use of a consumers' personal information. The guidelines require that the automobile industry use advanced encryption techniques and limit how they store and share data.[11] While these regulations could increase the cost of development, it's a good way to mitigate the potential risks involved.

Smart cars are on the rise and almost every automaker has either released a smart car or are planning to. Therefore, being the victim of an attack is no longer a matter of if, it's a matter of when the hack will occur and how serious it will be.[3] In a recent survey of auto engineers and IT professionals, 84% expressed concern that automakers weren't keeping pace with the industry's rapidly changing security threats.[1] Subsequently, 62% said their organizations don't have the cybersecurity skills needed to protect themselves and another 63% said that they test less than half of the hardware, software, and other technologies for vulnerabilities.[1] Unfortunately, as we'll come to see in this chapter, if the proper precautions aren't taken, smart car attacks can be a matter of life or death. If we want to make progress protecting our data in the auto industry, we need to lock more than our car doors.

While it's easy to understand the potential problems, we don't actively think about these "what if" scenarios when driving around because they're not saturating the news—yet. However, if we take a deeper look into the auto industry, we see that concerns are being actively expressed. At the basic level, hackers can get into your car and use the connectivity to access your private information or even steal your car.[2] But if we look at worst-case-scenario, a hacker could completely take over the control of your car—steering, gas, breaks, door locks—and cause a fatal accident.

Automotive hacking goes back decades. Even though technology wasn't as advanced, it was still possible to override the system. In 2010, a disgruntled former employee at the Texas Auto Center in Austin used a co-worker's account information to gain access to company software used for car repossession.[3] He went on to disable over 100 automobiles and the owners of these automobiles, who were up to date on payments, all went outside to discover their vehicles honking furiously and unable to start.[3]

In 2015, one of the highest-profile car hackings to-date occurred. It was carried out by security researchers in a controlled setting to address the concerns of automotive vulnerabilities. They hacked into a 2014 Jeep Cherokee to show how they could infiltrate the system and control steering, brakes, and the transmission—all from a laptop that was miles away.[1] They proceeded to take over the steering, disable the brakes, and shut down the engine.[2] This led to Fiat Chrysler recalling 1.4 million automobiles and trucks in an effort to beef up security.[3] Shortly after this incident, a hacker developed a low-cost device that could find, unlock, and remotely start any General Motors car that had OnStar communications installed.[3] This hacker, similar to those who took over the Jeep Cherokee, was a "white hat" hacker who's intent was to help the car company discover vulnerabilities in their system. On both occasions, no virulent activity occurred.

In 2018 alone, there were more than 60 documented automotive-related cybersecurity incidents, a six-fold increase in four short years.[3] One of these cybersecurity incidents occurred when an Australian man hacked into the database of the car-sharing start-up company GoGet. He hacked into more than 30 automobiles linked in the company and took 30 joy rides before he was arrested.[2] Not only can hackers access the automobiles; they can access the institutions behind the automobiles and any company that's associated with the car. This leads to even more cybersecurity problems and vulnerabilities for a breach of the car company's servers.

These automotive-related cybersecurity incidents have encouraged "white hat" hackers to come forward, find vulnerabilities, and work with manufacturers to create a better product. In one example, a "white hat" hacker took a drive in a 2017 Chevrolet and found that it collected his precise location, stored his phones ID and the people he called, and judged his acceleration and braking style to send real-time reports to General Motors.[8] This means that during the whole drive, there was an ongoing Internet connection tracking, analyzing, and storing his data.

Tesla automobiles are examples of the implications of futuristic technology that we can expect in more smart cars over the upcoming years. Currently, Tesla automobiles hold more data than most other smart cars due to their unique technological advancements. The computers on Tesla's store everything that a driver has voluntarily stored on their car, plus tons of other information generated by the vehicle itself such as video, location, navigational data, and even specific pre-crash information.[4] One problem with this is that crashed Tesla's are often sold at junk yards and auctions without being wiped of the data first. They're sold to the highest bidder and contain deeply personal, unencrypted data.[4] In an instance in 2018, a "white hat" hacker bought a Tesla Model 3 at an auction to conduct some research. He found that the Tesla's computer had stored data from at least 17 different devices and none of this data was encrypted.[4] Mobile phones or tablets had paired to the car around 170 times and it held 11 phonebooks' worth of contact information from both drivers and passengers who had previously connected their devices.[4] It also held calendar appointments, emails, and the last 73 navigational locations, which included residential addresses.[4] The Tesla computer recorded video footage the crash that totaled the car, which was stored in the computer.[5] It was learned that this car was owned by a construction company who allowed their employees to use it during work or for appointments.

In addition to an increase in car technology, we've seen more apps that can be connected to your smart car to increase convenience. For example, if you can unlock and start your car using an app, and you do so regularly, you're putting yourself at a higher risk. All a hacker needs to do to gain control of your vehicle is hack into the application itself.[2] The same can happen with GPS tracker apps. A hacker recently broke into thousands of accounts who were using two different GPS tracker applications—iTrack and ProTrack.[6] He gained access to 7,000 iTrack accounts and over 20,000 ProTrack accounts to expose vulnerabilities of these apps.[6] When he gained access, he was able to monitor the locations of thousands of vehicles and even turn off the engines for automobiles that were stopped or traveling 12 mph or slower.[6] He continued to say that while he could kill the engine's on all of these automobiles, he had no intent of doing so because it would be very dangerous.[6] Instead, he just wanted to show security vulnerabilities for apps that can be connected to your car's computer system.

All of the successful hacking attempts show us the vulnerabilities that come with an increase of smart car technology. Luckily, while we've seen the possibilities, most of the people infiltrating these smart cars are doing so to help the auto industry rather than harm them. These "white hat" hackers are exposing vulnerabilities so that they can be fixed, not profited upon. If action isn't taken, this could change. What's concerning is the amount of people that know they're making coding errors or security vulnerabilities and aren't doing anything to fix it. Automotive manufacturers aren't as cybersecurity savvy as they need to be. When surveyed, about 55% of IT security practitioners and engineers admitted to making coding errors and another 60% acknowledged that this lack of understanding in the industry and a lack of training on secure coding practices is a huge cause of vulnerabilities.[2] As more things become connected to the Internet, it's becoming more critical for automotive manufacturers to hire a cybersecurity expert to help with the design and development of smart car technology.

Think about the possibility of a criminal, terrorist, or even rogue government agent gaining secure access through a smart car.[3] Not only will this open up a treasure trove of information, but it can also be seriously dangerous to the lives of the drivers. When unauthorized remote access gains control of a vehicle's network, the potential for attackers to pivot to safety-critical systems risks not just the drivers' personal information, but their physical safety as well.[1] With the ability to hack into the controls system, someone could take control of your car and drive into a wall at 80mph or right off of a bridge. While we really hope that this isn't an action that potential hackers would be encouraged to do, the possibility is there and that's all that matters. As we saw with the 2014 Jeep Cherokee, it is possible for hackers to gain access to the steering, brake, and even transmission of a car. This could mean that criminals may try to ransom a vehicle, or its passengers, or thieves could direct and steer a car to a local chop-shop—with or without a passenger inside.[3]

Now, many people don't live their day-to-day lives with these concerns in the back of their minds, but it's still important to consider the capabilities of smart cars and what that means in worst-case-scenarios. What's more likely to happen are data breaches from seemingly innocent Bluetooth connections.

How many times have you gotten into a Bluetooth enabled rental car and immediately synced your phone to make hand free calls or access your music library? Chances are that you do this more times than not and you're not alone. The convenient smart technology that's now installed in almost all vehicles is often used without second thought. Nobody really thinks about the implications of this connectivity. But here's another question: how many times have you removed your synced device from the car when you're returning a rental? If you never do this, or have forgotten to before returning rentals, you're not alone. Millions of people return their rental cars without having disconnected their devices. This is why when you try to pair, you're often sitting there scrolling through 10 to 20 devices before you find yours to sync. Unfortunately, when you don't disconnect your phone from a rental car, you're giving hackers or malicious actors an open door into your data—and the amount of data transferred from a phone to a car is more surprising than you'd imagine. When you allow a car to access your phone, your phone's data is downloaded into the software and hardware of that car. Depending on how you have your phone set up, this could mean transferring bank codes, pin numbers for your ATM card, your contact list, your locations, or even access codes to your garage door. If you don't remove the phone from the software when you return the car, it stays accessible on the car's computer.

Even if you do disconnect your device, your phone's data is still on the car's hardware. This is a problem we need to address. There have been plenty of software advances in car technology and many institutions have incentives for "white hat" hackers to show them weaknesses in their systems. However, there's still no way for you to wipe the hardware of a car that's in use without creating some kind of removable disk that can be transferred with each new renter, leaser, or owner. Whether you rent or buy a car, when you download your phone inadvertently or on purpose, that car then contains all of your information. If the wrong people hack the information in your car, you're in big trouble; your data and your security is in big trouble. It can be accessed by the next person that rents the car you rented, the next person that leases the car you returned, or the next person that buys a car you just brought to a used car lot. This has become such an ordeal that the U.S. Federal Trade Commission has issued advisories to drivers warning them about pairing their devices with rental cars and urging them to learn how to wipe their car's software system clean of their personal data prior to returning them or selling a car they own.[4]

While people think that you need to have extremely technological or IT skills to hack into this information, it's a lot easier than you think. For example, Brendan recently bought a car that someone had owned before him. He was a doctor in Chicago and had only owned this car for about 45 days. So, Brendan bought the car and was driving home. When he went to connect his phone so he could use the Bluetooth, he realized that all of this guy's data was still on the car. Brendan started looking at it, not from a nefarious perspective, but just to see what's on there and he realized something pretty eye-opening. Brendan could access his home address, all of his contact phone numbers, his text messages, his driver's license and social security number, and more. Since Brendan had no malicious intent, he simply hit the delete button, but that's not what everyone would do. This can happen all the time when renting automobiles, leasing automobiles, or buying automobiles.

A promising shift we've seen in the auto industry is an increase in transparency about safety efforts. More and more automakers are going public with their efforts to make automobiles safe.[1] Mitsubishi has developed specific cyber defense technology for connected automobiles that offers multi-layered defense through a variety of robust security features.[9] Tesla has also released initiatives that encourage "white hat" hackers to find vulnerabilities and communicate them with Tesla directly so they can be fixed. Tesla routinely pays out five-figure sums to individuals who successfully find these flaws and report them in the correct way, as outlined by their guidelines.[4] While most of the car hackers that we've seen, or heard about, have been wearing "white hats" and haven't hacked into automobiles with any criminal intent, it shows us that we're still vulnerable. Because of this, automakers have banded together and formed the Automotive Information Sharing and Analysis Center, also known as Auto-ISAC.[3] This industry aims to "share and analyze intelligence about emerging cybersecurity risks to vehicles, and to collectively enhance vehicle cybersecurity capabilities across the global automotive industry, including light- and heavy-duty vehicle OEMs, supplies, and the commercial vehicle sector."[10]

It's a step in the right direction, but there are still no federal laws that dictate what kind of data the auto industry collects, how it's collected, or what is done after it's been collected and analyzed. Even Tesla, who encourages "white hat" hackers to find vulnerabilities in their systems, isn't transparent about the data that they're recording and storing on their internal systems.[4] People spend thousands of dollars to buy these smart cars, but then the data that it produces about you doesn't belong to you.[8] Most automobiles sold in the United States in 2021 will have built-in Internet connections either freely accessible or as an add-on feature.[8] Now, automobiles aren't just computers on wheels, they're also smartphones on wheels. When you utilize these Internet connections, you're giving consent to send and receive data from apps, insurance firms, and anything else the automaker sees fit.[8] In the fine print, some brands even reserve the right to use the data to track you down if you don't pay your bills.[8] What's worse is that most automakers actually go above and beyond to hide what kind of data they're collecting and sharing using complicated privacy policies that are written in legal jargon undecipherable by the everyday buyer.[8] By using OnStar, for example, you're giving the company the rights to a broad set of personal and driving data that lacks any detail regarding when or how often this data is collected.[8] They go as far as to say: "We may keep the information we collect for as long as necessary."[8] This means even after you sell your car, or discontinue using OnStar, they can keep your data and use it as they see fit. For Tesla's, you can opt out of data collection, but then you lose a bunch of the functionality features that make the brand unique.[4]

The California Consumer Privacy Act is starting to be enforced and has encouraged many other states, and federal agencies, to reconsider their data protection laws. This will place restrictions on data collection and require consent in a language that the consumer actually understands. Still, we have a long way to go before we can ensure that our data is being protected on smart cars. We need to start looking more closely at what happens to the data when we use a rental, when our car is sold as a used vehicle, when we replace tech with new devices, or when the car reaches its end of life. Where does all of the data go? Many people know how important it is to protect digital data on phones, laptops, tables, and other electronic devices. It's time we started treating our automobiles the same way. With Brendan's example of deleting the previous owner's information on his new car, it's important to remember something. Even though he hit the delete button and the data was no longer accessible on the interface of the car, the data still lives on the hard drive. For better automotive cybersecurity, we can't focus solely on the software side of things. For the most secure data protection, we'd need to figure out how to have removable hardware that can be taken and destroyed between owners. With more car companies facing liability for cybersecurity options, only a few have taken initiative to address the hardware side of this problem. There are a number of car companies that have turned to ERI for solutions and many of them have become ERI clients. We are also in negotiation with many others. ERI is proud to work with the automakers of our country to ensure that data is destroyed when a car has reached its end of life rather than thrown into a junkyard. As software data protection continues to rise in awareness, we can't leave hardware protection behind.

To further protect yourself, keep your software up to date, exercise caution when pairing devices with your vehicle, and keep your car secure. Always opt for strong passwords and make sure that you reset your car to factory settings when selling it or returning it to a rental.

Chapter 16: The 4G to 5G Switchover... We Ain't Seen Nothing Yet!!!

As technology has continued to advance, we've seen the transformation of wireless communication standards advance as well. From the moment that cell phones were released, cellular wireless technology has been needed. Phones connect to these signals so they can broadcast signals from cell towers back to your phones. The strength and speed of the signal depends on the technology. When phones were first introduced, we had 1G. 1G only had the capability of handling voice calls. Then, in the 1980s, we advanced to 2G technology, which allowed for data transfer as well as voice calls. This is when we started to see basic SMS messages and voicemail capabilities on mobile phones, but still no access to a mobile Internet.

What many of us remember is the introduction of 3G. This was a turning point in cellular capabilities. 3G advanced the ability to send and receive data with speeds up to 2 Mbps, which meant that we could send large emails and run Internet searches. 3G also enabled image sharing and even location-tracking technology for those who were able to access GPS on their phones. This created a huge increase in consumer's buying habits, as everyone just had to get the newest phone. People flooded into shops and almost overnight, everyone was using a 3G compatible phone. The latest technology that many of today's consumers have access to and use is 4G technology. 4G increased the speeds at which people used the Internet and sent or received messages and photos. It also enabled an entire economy of apps that required reliable connectivity. 4G introduced video calling on cell phones and made it possible for phones to perform almost all of the same functions of a computer. When people realized this, the same thing happened with the consumer market—everyone needed the newest model.

People threw aside their 3G phones so they could rush out to buy the newest 4G compatible model and enjoy all of the convenience that came with it. Wireless Internet capabilities changed our lives and made it possible to do so much more in so many facets of life—at home, at work, or even while exploring the great outdoors.[4] It's become so second nature, that many of us don't even think about it until the Wi-Fi goes out or we're in an area with no service. Now, we're about to experience another huge transformation in how we use and share data.

The 4G to 5G switchover is going to be one of the biggest, most impactful transitions in history and we don't think people understand the magnitude of what's going to happen. It's going to be far bigger than the switch from analog to digital and bigger than black-and-white to color. It's a huge change that impacts not only cell phones, but any electronic device that has 4G compatibility. 4G speeds were fast and they had supporting hardware or technology with the capacity to process data. With a switchover to 5G, these devices all become obsolete. This means routers, modems, even automobiles with 4G—things far past simple cell phones—will all need to be replaced. We'll go into more detail on this later, but first it's important to understand the basics of what 5G is and the effects that it will have on the world as we know it.

When looking at how 5G technology works, you need to understand the types of frequencies that are required to allow such enhanced performance capabilities. 5G works on different frequencies across the low-, mid-, and high-band specturm.[1] They work with sub-6 GHz and millimeter-wave (20-60 GHz) frequencies,[1] which come with a few technological hurdles. For one, millimeter-wave (mmWave) is an extremely high-frequency—with some reports reaching up to 300 GHz[2]—which means that the wavelengths can't travel very far.[1] These mmWave frequencies are so sensitive, they can't pass through many windows or buildings unless the 5G nodes are extremely close together.[1] To ensure that 5G is actually effective and can be implemented on a widespread level, networks need to pair the mmWaves with the sub-6 GHz.[1] This helps address the problem mmWave's distance capabilities. In contrast, 4G frequencies are much lower—below 5 GHz. Because of these differences, we can't just transfer the connection to the current 4G towers that are erected across the world. We need to build new 5G towers that can handle the higher frequency and that are positioned closer together. The higher the frequency of a wave, the more data that can be transmitted from one device to another, but the shorter this data can travel.[13] We'll need to install many more towers than what we have now and update outdated ones with the new technology. Currently, the United States has about 215,000 cell towers.[13] For national coverage, we're going to need anywhere from 1 million to 2.1 million additional 5G towers.[13]

Another key difference is that 5G frequencies are much more directional than 4G.[2] 4G frequencies emit data all over, so they can be picked up randomly by other towers. While you'd think that this might be effective, it actually wastes power and energy and can structurally weaken access to the Internet.[2] The directionality of 5G allows for the most precise wireless communications we've seen in technology to date.

5G boasts a low latency, high bandwidth transfer of data. This means that the time it takes for a 5G signal to travel is a mere fraction of what 4G was capable of. Not only will websites load faster, but you'll also experience higher download speeds, virtually no lagging, and an all-new way to use immersive technology. 5G has the potential to be 20 times faster than 4G. Currently, 4G download speeds peak at 1 Gbps—5G will peak at 20 Gbps,[2] with many people experiencing an average of 10 Gbps. For 5G to work best, towers need to be consistent across locations, which means that we'll start to see more rural connectivity than ever before. According to the discussions happening now, 4G and 5G are going to coexist.[1] This way, if you happen to lose 5G signal, it will fall back on the 4G LTE that's still in use. As we continue to transition into a more 5G world, this dual connectivity is important to address any initial weaknesses in the system.

In short, the application of 5G technology is going to affect everyone and will lead to tremendous changes in how we go about our lives. With broadband speeds up to 20 Gbps, you'll be able to download a two-hour movie in 3.6 seconds.[13] That's fast, especially when compared to the six minutes that it currently takes on 4G.[13] Not jaw dropping enough? Using 5G, you could theoretically download every single movie and TV show that's currently on Netflix in under 24 hours.[13] That's unthinkable with our current technology, but thanks to the low latency that 5G brings, it's possible—albeit probably quite unnecessary.

With such low latency capabilities, 5G will allow for improvements in augmented reality (AR), virtual reality (VR), robotics development, autonomous vehicles (AVs), cloud gaming, immersive education, and healthcare applications.[2] We can expect 5G to open up possibilities for advancements in automobile technology and medical technology that we haven't yet seen. 5G is going to completely revolutionize and transform the Internet of Things as we know it. When you combine augmented reality with virtual reality, we could see a 100% transformation of the educational system. Imagine using both AR and VR to bring concepts in textbooks alive so that children in classrooms can learn through immersive experience rather than merely conceptually.[1] An interior design company could use their VR technology to show a customer what changes would look like in their own home. They could immediately change furniture, layouts, paint colors, window treatments, and even the pictures in the picture frames using 5G technology. Financial services could transform ATMs into full-service branches powered by video conference.[2] We'll see a complete elimination of lags or stutters on video connections, and you won't experience the annoying occurrence of apps freezing on your phone. 5G could even have the potential to eliminate the motion sickness that some people experience when using VR and AR.[5] Smart cities will work more efficiently and offer instantaneous information transference. Data will be easily captured from remote sensors, transferred to data centers, and applied to AI and data science for real-time analyses.[14]

Autonomous cars will become a very real part of life as they could use live maps for real-time navigation and drastically reduce the current safety issues being discussed.[2] The low latency capabilities that come with 5G mean that vehicle-to-vehicle and vehicle-to-infrastructure communication will reach the levels they need to be to make autonomous driving a reality.[13] This instant communication will allow autonomous cars to avoid collisions and even correct traffic patterns.[13] This is the difference between life and death when traveling in an self-driving vehicle.

At the core of it, everything is going to have immersive capabilities and our technology will be faster and more responsive than ever imagined. We're likely going to start seeing a shift of technology that uses cues from our surroundings or individual circumstances to activate ads, personalize electronics, and even autonomously react for us. This will lead to benefits for all industries across the board, especially retail. The increase in effectiveness of signal transfers also means better energy savings and lower long-term consumer costs. At the base level, 5G is creating possibilities that we have yet to even imagine.

Since these changes in technology are so much different than the current 4G, we're not going to see things happen overnight. With the introduction of 5G technology, all of our electronics and wireless connections are going to change. We have to expect that this will take time. We anticipate seeing the major changes happening in about five years with most electronics carrying 5G capabilities in seven years. Many experts agree with this and predict that there will be about 200 million 5G connections by the end of 2021 with numbers growing to 2.8 billion 5G connections by 2025.[1] These estimated connections include all devices, not just cell phones. However, cell phones are likely going to be the first things to change.

While some carriers are starting to test 5G in certain areas, we're still in a transitional period. For instance, AT&T

rolled out a faster version of 4G LTE that wasn't quite 5G speeds and labeled it 5Ge.[4] This isn't the same as 5G, although AT&T does have "real" 5G connections in the works. One thing that everyone agrees on in terms of 5G —it's extremely fast. As we saw with the examples above, 5G is faster than we could have ever imagined. As it continues to gain traction in the news, many carriers are starting to unveil their plans for rolling out 5G on a nationwide level.

On December 10, 2019, the FCC auctioned off a large portion of mmWaves that communication companies will need to support 5G and all corresponding electronics.[9] For this to be possible, the FCC created the Rural Digital Opportunity Fund, which will work to provide $20.4 billion worth of subsidies over 10 years to eligible institutions who are willing to build out fiber lines for 5G in underserved, rural areas.[9] Doing this will help 5G reach a national level and serve more of the population. However, this is only a portion of the funds that are going to be needed for a complete rollout. It's estimated that the U.S. needs a total of $80 billion to complete a nation-wide 5G rollout, so the FCC's funds are still insufficient.[11] The Rural Digital Opportunity Fund will help create networks that will last for years to come and prioritize higher network speed and lower latency.[10] This initiative is part of the FCC's 5G Fast Plan, which aims to make the U.S. the global leader in 5G technologies.[9]

The FCC 5G Fast Plan, released in December 2019, was an effort to push 5G rollout into high gear.[12] In this plan, regulations will be updated to support 5G expansion, more low-, mid-, and high-band spectrum will be released into the market, and policies will be altered to speed up small-cell technology construction.[12] While this means that we can fully expect 5G to become more prevalent in 2021, there's still a lot to do. More realistically, this plan will be unveiled across the U.S., and the world, over a five to 10-year timeline.

In the meantime, many cellular carriers are starting to make the switch to 5G on their own. All of the major carriers currently have some sort of 5G phone and 5G data plan available, but most of the data plans are only available in certain markets. We currently have half-a-dozen 5G-capable smartphones available on the market and this number is only expected to rise.[1] All of the major carriers currently offer at least one type of 5G smart phone and nearly all of the phone manufacturers have released one model—some are already starting to produce 5G-connected laptops.[1] While many phone carriers are only releasing their 5G network in certain markets, additional service locations are going to be added throughout the year. This has spurred a bit of an arms race between big telecom and tech companies, as well as global state powers.[6] As we continue to experience the 5G takeover, there are some questions that need to be answered.

As we briefly discussed in the beginning of this chapter, the switchover from 4G to 5G is going to require a lot more than changing out a few cell towers. Since so much technology was developed to be compatible with 4G—routers, modems, televisions, smart appliances, cell phones, and more—this technology is soon going to be obsolete. 4G devices will not have the capacity to run on 5G networks, so all of these technologies will have to be upgraded to 5G if you want to enjoy the benefits that 5G has to offer. This isn't going to happen immediately, but we anticipate that this switchover will start as early as this year and continue on for the next five to seven years or more. This means two different things. One, all of your devices are going to become even more interconnected than they already are, which increases the risk of cyberattacks. Two, all of the old electronics are going to need to be disposed of in some way or another. Let's explore the issues with cybersecurity first.

Every single piece of new technology faces some sort of obstacle along the way—it's inevitable. Even if the hardware is securely manufactured, once software goes live and people begin to increase the connectivity of their lives, we'll need to be careful about our data protection. As we've seen in recent chapters, the technology we have now already causes problems and the federal government has been slow to implement a nation-wide solution. This will become even more problematic with 5G.

When 4G networks were released, there was a lot of disruption to the industry and we started to realize the potential reach of malicious hackers.[15] While 5G offers a lot of innovative advancements in technology, it also means that there is a higher risk of use for the average consumer. 5G means more traffic, more connected devices, and more opportunity for hackers.[15] If more technology relies on the low latency benefits of 5G, it means that there will be little to no room for error. Experts are saying that while 5G is new, the problem isn't going to arise from the network itself. Instead, we're going to see an increased risk because of the rise of connectivity between devices and the Internet.[16] 5G will undoubtedly cause a sharp increase regarding the Internet of Things and it's estimated that the number of Internet-connected items will grow from the current 14.2 billion to about 25 billion devices by 2021 alone.[16] The problem here is that once hackers get into a device, they'll be able to gain access to any other devices that's connected to the network. This opens up a treasure trove of information. Consumers can reduce their chances of a breach by always encrypting their data, using strong passwords, and keeping their devices up to date with the latest security software.

In addition to an increase in risk to our data protection on the software side of the 5G switchover, we're also going to see a huge increase in risk to data stored on hardware of old devices. When you get rid of your old electronics and don't recycle it properly, you're giving hackers an open door to your personal, sensitive information. With the amount of interconnectivity, this could lead hackers right back into your active devices, giving them control of every single electronic you own and use along with all of the data that's stored in those devices. John was with one of ERI's carrier clients who drove this point home. In a conversation, our client told John that between the big carriers in the industry, they have about a trillion routers that they're going to need to recycle as 5G takes over. One trillion routers made of metals and plastics and sensitive data, and that's just **one** type of item... Now think about how many cell phones, computers, tablets, fitness wearables, smart cars, smart appliances, home security systems, and every other 4G electronic that's on the market today. That's a lot of electronics that are going to need to be responsibly recycled. 5G is going to stimulate electronic replacement rates like we've never seen, and we need to be ready to put a plan in place to responsibly react to that.

As our "tech-hungry" nation begins to upgrade all of its devices, we're going to see potentially disastrous effects on the environment from improperly discarded electronics. Our society is drawn to having the new, best products so we'll start to see a lot of people discarding their 4G compatible phones that are in perfect condition, in lieu of a 5G capable device. It will be almost a forced turnover, as people won't be able to access certain things on their old devices. This would be fine if we responsibly recycle our electronics. In fact, it could actually help proliferate the circular economy and lead to better, more efficient manufacturing. Sadly, the reality is that less than a quarter of the e-waste consumed in the U.S. is recycled. Instead, it ends up in landfills, ripe for the picking or ready to emit harmful byproducts as it degrades. This is going to get worse with 5G not only due to electronic turnover, but the simultaneous rise of the Internet of Things. With the speeds that 5G offers, everything is going to have 5G signal. Vehicle tracking, airplane tracking, even tracking luggage at the airport is going to begin, which means more electronics are going to be produced and eventually, need to be updated or replaced. In conjunction with 5G rollout, we're starting to see a new generation in other networks as well. Wi-Fi 6 is on the rise along with Bluetooth 5—both of which contribute to the coming hyperconnected era.[4] With all of the new technology, it's no surprise that our e-waste problem is expected to grow.

Moving forward, as we continue to navigate through the decade, the biggest thing we'll need to focus on from 2021 to 2030 is how 5G will impact data destruction and e-waste. One way to improve the problem is to start making electronics that last and can be upgraded via software or small replacement parts. A push towards a circular economy will help protect data and reduce the electronic waste that ends up in our landfills. If a phone battery starts to die, we should have an option to simply replace the battery rather than replace the entire phone. Unfortunately, the U.S. as a whole tends to resist change—especially when big institutions are profiting so much. On a personal level, we can start actively seeking electronics recycling plants that are certified and offer data destruction. Check and see if your city or town has a drop-off center for e-waste or try going back to the retailer where you bought your phone. If you find a local recycling plant, make sure that they have the proper certifications, like e-Stewards, R2, and NAID, so that your data is 100% destroyed and electronics aren't shipped to a developing country. ERI offers a number of electronics waste recycling programs and has eight facilities across the country. While we'll need a more wide-spread effort to make a true difference, we can all do our part to protect our data and the environment.

Chapter 17: Gone Remote – Hardware Security Concerns of Remote Employees and Their Electronics

While the industries we discussed in the previous chapters are those most frequently plagued with cybersecurity problems, they're not an exclusive group. Any organization can experience data breaches in any industry. In the past, smaller businesses in less sensitive industries weren't targeted as much, but with the rise of remote working capabilities, hackers are starting to give them more attention than ever.

The term "remote workers" can apply to a number of industries. There are possibilities for security concerns if the healthcare, financial, retailers, military, or auto industry use remote workers. This chapter covers security concerns with all remote work, regardless of the industry. If you're allowing your employees to work remotely and handle sensitive information, it's even more important to make sure that you're taking the proper precautions to secure client or patient data.

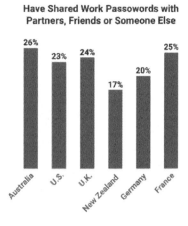

Over the past 10 years, remote work has become more attractive to employees and businesses alike. With remote work, businesses often see a rise in productivity while simultaneously reducing overhead costs. Not only that, but employee satisfaction skyrockets and turnover is drastically diminished. They're able to scout talent that may not be in their physical area and give their employees a better work-life balance. At the same time, employees are loving it. Remote work reduces the need to commute and gives employees more control over their daily lives. Before the beginning of COVID-19, only 29% of Americans were able to work from home regularly,[5] while 90% of the workforce admitted to working remotely at least once. During the height of the outbreak and the shelter-in-place initiatives, almost all employees became remote workers. Now, after getting a taste of what that means, 99% of workers would choose to work remotely if they could, for at least part of the time, for the remainder of their careers.[5] When surveyed, 80% of U.S. workers now say they would turn down a job that didn't offer at least some sort of remote working capabilities.[2] With this in mind, it's expected that a majority of workforces are going to transform into positions that can be done remotely.

Remote work is a win-win for everyone, but it also creates a serious problem. Cybersecurity risk prevention has not increased at the same rate as remote working opportunities.[3] There are tons of security lapses that occur with remote work and without the proper precautions in place, this leads to an increase in data breaches and malicious attacks. Mobile workforces have the potential to completely change the way we look at data security and we need to make sure that we're taking these scenarios into considerations sooner rather than later. 86% of senior leadership teams agreed that data breaches are more likely to occur when employees are working out of the office.[6] What's more is that 57% of CIOs have suspected that their current mobile workforce has been hacked at some point over the past 12 months.[6] About a quarter of the businesses who allow remote work possibilities don't have any sort of antivirus or cybersecurity software installed on the devices and 30% don't restrict remote access to company files in any way.[4] As we'll come to see, both of these things are extremely important to protecting the privacy and data of a business' constituents.

As a way to increase the protection against cyberattacks during the influx of remote workers due to the coronavirus pandemic, the Cybersecurity and Infrastructure Security Agency (CISA) released some new guidelines. The interim Trusted Internet Connection 3.0 is a telework guidance that addresses different scenarios where federal employees would need to connect remotely.[7] It encourages agencies to implement several security controls related to tracking the use of agency devices, incident response, intrusion detection, and adds two new policy enforcement points: data protection and unified communications and collaboration.[7] These measures are meant to decrease the risk of telework by preventing data exfiltration and ensuring the privacy and integrity of the data being accessed.[7]

When we consider remote work, it's fairly straightforward to see how cybersecurity problems are more prevalent. Remote workers have access to a range of servers, data, databases, email, or cloud computing systems from their laptops or mobile devices.[2] For organizations that allow remote work, also referred to as "telework," they also allow contractors, business partners, vendors, and other third parties to access information from remote locations.[1] This includes all components of technologies that aren't being used under the roof of the organization itself. The more remote access they allow, the greater the risk that the organization experiences a data security breach or compromises their information in some way. When their devices are at a higher risk, the risk to the internal servers grows proportionally—especially when there are no preventative systems in place to protect sensitive data.

Think about it this way. If an employee was sitting at Starbucks working off of the public Wi-Fi network, a malicious actor could easily gain access to that person's computer. From here, they can gain access to any documents that are on the computer or connected to the organization's network. Even if the organization's network was secured, the hacker could access the remote worker's email to send phishing emails or other contaminated content to their trusted network of contacts.[2] If you got an email from a fellow coworker or even high-up executive, you're more likely to click it and succumb to an attack. Now, even though the malicious actor didn't have direct access to the internal network on the remote device, they've created a doorway into the secure server system that's located in the office. This is just one example of the cybersecurity risks to remote employees.

As remote work has continued to shift and become a more permanent part of our daily lives, we've started to see more gaps in security. While there are plenty of security measures that have been enacted by institutions who now require remote work, a lot of it relies on employee understanding and knowing what to do when things go wrong.[8] Due to this rapid shift, the gaps in security have been exacerbated and hackers have an easier way in. Many staff that work from home are distracted and have been falling for phishing scams more frequently. Cybercriminals have started preying on anxiety surrounding the coronavirus and have begun intensifying ransomware and DDoS attacks.[9] This started almost immediately. In March 2020, a Czech hospital that was serving as a COVID-19 testing center was hit with a cyberattack in the midst of the outbreak, forcing some services to shut down temporarily.[9] While the aim of many DDoS attacks is disruption, they have the potential to crumble a virtual network. Since these are relatively easy to carry out, the pandemic has brought out a plethora of attackers who are looking to cause chaos, disrupt organizations, or even extort campaigns.[9] We saw this firsthand with the hacks that disrupted thousands of Zoom classrooms around the country during the beginning of the lock-down.

Since the onset of COVID-19 we've seen a marked increase in cybercrime in general. The FBI's Internet Crime Complaint Center (IC3) has been receiving upwards of 3,000 - 4,000 complaints a day.[10] Prior to the pandemic, these numbers were closer to 1,000. While there are a lot of COVID-related complaints, there remain to be more general complaints than in the past.[10] Foreign hackers have been targeting U.S.-based COVID-19 research, supply chains have been disrupted, and fraudulent domains and events have popped up around the country.[10]

While a majority of people in the U.S. and beyond are still trying to find a way to do their part in containing the spread of COVID-19, it's created a landscape for cybercriminals to capitalize on. Instead of playing into these problems, it's important for institutions to take the necessary steps and issue mandatory training that shows their employees how to secure their remote work technology and software.

According to NASA, during the first week in April 2020, email phishing attempts doubled, there was an exponential increase in malware attacks on NASA systems, and there were twice as many mitigation-blocking of NASA systems trying to access malicious sites due to users accessing the Internet from remote locations.[11] Due to these increases in cyberattacks, it's estimated that cybercrime **will** cost the world $6 trillion by the end of 2021.[12] This staggering number equates to higher profits than all of the major illegal drug trades combined.[12]

The government has issued warnings, enacted temporary laws and agencies to help control the influx of cyberattacks, and has given advice as to how to avoid falling victim to COVID-19 related cyberattacks. The best way to protect yourself and your company is to make sure that you and your employees are practicing awareness and never open any email that you're unsure of.

To elaborate, most of the concerns that revolve around remote work include the lack of physical security controls that come with working inside a designated office, the use of unsecured networks, the connection of infected devices to internal networks, and the availability of internal resources to external hosts.[1] Remote work involves the use of employee devices such as personal desktop or laptop computers, smartphones, and tablets to perform their jobs.[1] These devices may be owned by the business and used for working at home, owned by a third-party, or even personal devices of the employee themselves. The way that they can gain access to the resources of their organization involves remotely accessing data in one of four ways. Organizations allow their employees to gain remote access through tunneling, portals, remote desktop access, or direct application access. Depending on your organization, one of these methods may be better than the other, so it's important to understand your security needs prior to moving forward with a method of access.

Tunneling is when an organization offers a secure communications tunnel where information can be transmitted between networks.[1] Tunnels are usually created using virtual private network (VPN) technology.[1] Using a tunnel, information is protected using cryptography, authentication checkpoints, access control, and other critical security features. However, they fail to provide protection for communication between the VPN gateway and internal resources.[1] To make sure that the network is secure, it's important to block off parts of the network and different types of access that come after authentication is confirmed.[1]

Application portals are similar to VPNs, but they're web-based and rely on a portal to connect the remote worker to the organization's resources. The security features are similar to tunnels, but the application client software and associated data are stored inside of the portal server rather than on the client device.[1] This allows for a stronger control over how the data is secured and limits access to certain applications outside of the internal network. There are web-based portals or terminal server access portals, depending on the needs of your organization's remote work. The most secure application portal is a virtual desktop infrastructure (VDI), which helps to safeguard remote work done using personal devices or devices that are operated by a third-party.[1] The differences between all of the application portals are how each of them stores data, either temporarily or permanently.

Remote desktop access allows workers to remotely control a particular computer within the organization.[1] For telecommuters, this means they're able to login to their desktop or their work computer using their personal device. Therefore, remote workers can gain access to everything that's on their computer in the office either directly or indirectly. Most direct remote desktops are prevented by firewalls, so many people opt for indirect access through a trusted intermediate system.[1] To eliminate any cybersecurity problems with an intermediate system, it's important to thoroughly evaluate the security provided and any possible data breaches that could occur by using a third-party system. The better you identify potential problems, the more likely you are to successfully mitigate them in the future.

The last type of remote access is direct application access. This can be used without remote access software by working on a specific application directly.[1] The app will have its own security an authentication process and is usually hosted through either an HTTP or HTTPS address.[1] Since this type of remote work is the most susceptible to cyberthreats, it's important to only access data over secure networks when other security measures have been taken.

With all of the remote work options available, it becomes apparent how data breaches occur. If devices are using an unsecured network, hackers can gain access to whatever data is present or manipulated on an employee's computer—even if it's done as securely as possible. When hackers gain access to an employee's personal device, getting into the internal network is easy. The problem is that personal devices aren't usually secured as thoroughly as work computers, so to mitigate the risks of cybersecurity, you have to place an emphasis on malware and cybersecurity software. Before allowing any remote work to be conducted, you need to develop a system that can model potentially dangerous data breach scenarios. This allows you to identify loopholes and create procedures for action that would need to be taken in the event of a breach. Cybersecurity is a proactive measure and needs to be planned and implemented before a new program is launched. That means that businesses should just assume that their employees' remote devices will be hacked into. This way, you can stay one step ahead of problems.

If your business works in highly sensitive information, it's important to weigh the risks and the benefits of allowing remote work. If you can't justify allowing access to the entire internal network, there are ways to limit access and safeguard sensitive information.

There are a number of new threats that come with remote work, all of which mean you'll need added layers of protection. First, there's a lack of physical security to the information.[1] If your employees are using devices outside of your office, this means that they can carry it around with them. This is very convenient for people wanting more flexibility in their work, but it also increases the chances of an employee losing the device or having it stolen. To safeguard the information from physical threats, make sure that everything is encrypted so that it can't be recovered by unauthorized parties easily.[1] If that's not possible, consider simply not storing any sensitive information on the device at all and always use two-factor authentication.

Another major threat is the use of unsecured networks. To mitigate these threats, use firewalls and various types of malware or cybersecurity software. There should be a clear protocol for using external devices in the office to avoid any chance of introducing infected devices to the internal network.[1] The best way to avoid this is to use a separate network for all external devices, even when they're present in the office. By creating a separate, external, dedicated network for remote workers to use within your organization's server, you'll reduce any serious problems.[1] This could mean that the work is limited in nature, but it creates an extremely strong safeguard that could make all of the difference. It's also important to make sure that your employees are only using trusted hosts and not accessing sensitive information on public Wi-Fi networks. Two-factor authentication should be the bare minimum for access and all information should be encrypted when transferring between networks or being stored on a personal device. The main thing for organizations to keep in mind is that external environments are less controllable, so additional security measures are recommended.[1]

For the most control, manually secure all of the external devices that are going to be used. This means that employees will not be able to work from personal devices unless they've gone through all of the organizational requirements put in place to reduce the chances of cyber breaches. While this is more work upfront, it could save hundreds of thousands of dollars and increase data protection tremendously. As we've said, planning remote work with the realization that external environments have more hostile threats is a good starting point. From here, developing a security policy that defines all remote work requirements will help to strengthen the organization as a whole.[1] This might mean restricting access to only low-risk information, depending on your industry. All of the remote work done needs to follow strict protocol and security processes and devices need to undergo security upgrades and maintenance regularly.

Data protection loss software is a good thing to implement, as it controls what data outside of the internal server can be transferred and who it can be transferred to.[2]

As a whole, IT asset management is key. Every company needs to keep track of IT assets from the moment they're acquired until the moment it's confirmed that they've been destroyed—especially when utilizing remote employees. When IT assets aren't managed properly, it's easy to lose track and subject data to breaches. These practices need to be applied to any device being used outside of the office. This includes desktop computers, laptops, smartphones, fax machines, printers, and even copiers. Company policies need to be communicated thoroughly so that they're fully understood by remote workers. The best way to do this is during onboarding so that every employee knows how to protect their work and what they need to do in case of a data breach or loss or theft of a device. If any changes are made to these protocols, all employees should be notified in a timely manner.

The initiation and development of security protocols are crucial, but implementation is what protects the sensitive data within your organization. This includes ongoing work and the eventual disposal of any device that is no longer being used for work. Unfortunately, many institutions aren't taking the proper precautions for hardware destruction. This is even more concerning when employees who use personal devices need to dispose of it. When a remote employee accesses the business' server through a personal device and then recycles or throws away their electronics, all of that information is still stored on the hardware. To make sure this data doesn't fall into the wrong hands, you need to treat their personal computer or device as if it was part of your business. That means meeting the legal requirements for data destruction, sanitizing the media on the computer, and disposing the equipment properly.[1] ERI offers complete, secure data destruction to help you safeguard your company's data on any electronic device being used. Regardless of if you're using an in-house employee or remote workers, proper hardware related data destruction needs to be part of your security protocol.

Chapter 18: Hardware Data Destruction for Dummies—Yes, We Mean You

Throughout this book we've discussed data breaches in thorough detail. While a lot of the major information on these breaches focuses on software or servers, hardware data breaches are becoming more prevalent. With the rise of the Internet of Things and the switch from 4G to 5G, we're going to start seeing a sharp increase in data breaches from hardware and old electronics. The only way to protect data from outdated electronics is to ensure that the hardware is being destroyed the right way. Since roughly 40% of devices resold on publicly available resale channels contain personally identifiable information,[1] hardware destruction is more important than ever. In this day and age, hardware security is one of the best measures a company can take to prevent a breach.

Not only does responsibly recycling your electronics protect your sensitive information, but it also has tremendous benefits to the environment. When you properly recycle your electronics, you avoid contributing to the millions of tons of toxic items that end up in landfills that subsequently contaminate our food, water, and air. Creating a responsible hardware destruction plan will also save you and your organization millions of dollars in fines that are imposed after data breaches over time. Clearly, responsibly recycling old electronics is critically important.

With that being said, one of the things that most people and businesses struggle with is finding a responsible recycling plant that provides 100% data destruction while adhering to federal laws with environmentally friendly processes. The harder it is for people to find these corporations, the more likely they're going to give up and toss their old electronics in the garbage. To make this process easier, we're going to outline all of the things that you need to look for in a responsible e-waste recycling plant.

First, avoid hiring third party e-waste recyclers that seem too good to be true. If a recycler offers extremely cheap services or isn't able to give you a detailed description about what happens to your electronics, there's something else going on. Unfortunately, a lot of electronic recycling plants are still shipping their waste off to third world countries. According to a 2016 study, about one-third of e-waste produced in the U.S. was being sent overseas for processing. As we've discussed, this creates both environmental problems and data security problems. If there's any indication that the recycling company does this, run for the hills. Luckily, there are a few ways to be sure that this doesn't happen.

Ask how a recycling plant destroy the data on old electronics and whether or not the company can provide proof of destruction. You should also inquire about any certifications that the recycling company has. A reputable company should at least have a few of the certifications we'll discuss next. Since the federal government and EPA haven't provided a comprehensive national framework for e-waste legislation, there are several organizations that have created certifications in response.

You'll need to consider each e-waste certification that's currently recognized by professionals. The different certifications all mean something specific, but some of the top ones ensure that all of your electronic waste stays in North America to be processed and recycled responsibly. When a recycling company does not have these certifications, it's very likely that they ship their electronics to developing countries. You do not want your electronics being shipped to another country where they may be resold without your knowledge. The primary certifications include R2, e-Stewards, NAID AAA, ISO 19001, ISO 14001, and ISO 45001. The R2 certification and e-Stewards certification are two of the highest certifications you can gain in the e-waste industry. An R2 certification (Sustainable Electronics Recycling International's Responsible Recycling Standards for Electronics Recyclers) means that the recycling company is doing everything possible to keep employees safe and also guarantees that your electronics are recycled or repaired following a strict criterion where all steps are documented along the way. The e-Stewards certification ensures that a company does not ship any electronics out of North America. Instead, the e-waste recycler or ITAD company processes the items in the country using methods that help the environments.

The other main certificate to look for is the NAID (National Association for Information Destruction) AAA certification. This shows that a company is compliant with all data protection laws set forth by the International Secure Information Governance & Management Association (i-SIGMA). The NAID AAA certificate is only awarded to facilities that show their commitment to data security and destruction.

All of these certifications are only given to a recycling company after they've successfully passed a detailed audit through the associated agency. If a company is certified, you know that they are trustworthy and dedicated to quality. If the recycling company either doesn't have these certifications or won't show you the certificates, move on to the next company. When an e-waste or ITAD vendor is not certified, it's an indication that they have not been able to verify that they actually keep clients' data safe and dispose of electronic waste in a responsible manner. ERI holds all of the certifications listed above in addition to being a Microsoft Registered Refurbishing company and a partner in Homeland Security's STOP.THINK.CONNECT.™ public awareness campaign.

We recommend looking at the e-waste recycling company's experience next. The amount of time they've been in the business isn't exactly reflective of their quality. However, institutions that can back up their data destruction and protection of sensitive information with major clients and large institutions are a good sign. It shows you that they can be trusted, especially if they work with financial institutions or government agencies. With so many institutions who merely claim that they're eco-conscious and committed to data security, then turn around and dispose of electronics irresponsibly with no regards to your data, it's important to take the time to do your research. If the recycling company offers nationwide services, it's a good sign. Recycling institutions who offer coast-to-coast services have demonstrated that they're able to successfully expand geographically. This shows that their business model is highly trusted by their clients and they've been able to take that trust and grow their business as a result. ERI is the largest e-waste recycler in North America, and we have the infrastructure to serve clients in all 50 states. Our facilities are located in California, Washington, Indiana, Texas, Colorado, North Carolina, New Jersey, and Massachusetts. We're not saying that you must use ERI to recycle your electronics, but we want to make sure to provide you with characteristics and criteria to look for in general.

Finding a recycling company with transparency in their operations is one of the best ways to ensure that you're getting the services you need, without any potential problems regarding data protection. If there are any middlemen involved in the process of the electronic recycling, it increases exposure and risk. The more people that have access to your data, the greater the risk of a data breach. ERI processes all of our e-waste on our own without any outside help and we encourage all other recycling companies to do the same. One way to do this is to offer both on-site and off-site data destruction for a variety of industry needs. If your business holds sensitive information and has stringent processes for how data is protected, on-site destruction is a good option. This allows you to closely monitor the destruction of any sensitive or personally identifiable information without having to worry about who the data is with or if it's ever at risk of theft. On-site data destruction helps to solidify your peace of mind when it comes to containing sensitive data, which is understandable when you think about how many data breaches happen every day. If on-site data destruction is not available, make sure that you know exactly how your hard drives and other devices are handled in transit from your company to the electronics recycling and data destruction plant. See if the company offers the ability to watch the data destruction process remotely as an alternative. ERI allows our clients to choose their option—either on-site or off-site—and gives any client access to a live video feed of the recycling process if interested.

While on-site data destruction is a good option for increased security, it's not always the most effective choice. Large quantities of data are easier to destroy off-site in a secure facility and the process is less disruptive to overall business operations. Since on-site data destruction requires a large truck, it might not be feasible to certain businesses or clients who don't have the space. ERI offers four different levels of data destruction to ensure that your security levels match your needs.

We offer Standard Compliance, Enhanced Compliance, High Security, and Demilitarization so that you can rest easy knowing your data is in good hands and will be completely destroyed. For our clients increased comfort, we provide proof of data destruction through live feeds, video monitoring, and tracking capabilities.

Good recycling companies will give you a way to track your electronic waste as it moves through the recycling process. ERI uses proprietary Optech software for our clients to keep an eye on their electronics from start to finish. We give our clients the choice to watch the data being destroyed so they can witness it in real-time. For the ultimate security during data destruction, always choose a recycling facility that has monitored security alarms with motion detection, 24-hour video surveillance of entries and main areas, metal detectors at entries and exits, RFID cards and Proxy Ready entries and exits into secure areas of the facility, security gates on loading docks, and authorized personnel data destruction and asset management areas where only qualified, e-Verified employees have access. This sounds like a lot, but with data becoming more and more valuable, you need to take every precaution possible to ensure that your data is protected—even during the destruction process. ERI offers all of the above security features alongside custom protocols for any of your data destruction needs.

The next thing to check is the method of data destruction that the electronic recycling company uses. Some methods are better than others, so you want to make sure that the software is not only wiped, but the hardware is shredded as well. This leaves no chance of having the data ever be accessed again. After the device is shredded, the pieces can be separated into materials like metal or plastic, melted down, and reused to make new electronics that offer a clean slate for new data.

Finally, the last thing to check is whether or not the recycling company has a data breach response plan in place. While we hope that it wouldn't come to this, it's always good to prepare for the worst-case scenarios. Data breaches can severely damage a business, but you can limit that damage when you have a response plan in place. This plan needs to be thorough and well planned out. ERI's data breach response plan requires that the affected client be notified as soon as possible and calls for an immediate investigation into any suspected breach, even if a breach has not yet been confirmed. After investigating the incident, the client will receive a summary of exactly what happened, alongside how much and what type of information was compromised during the breach. Our data breach response plan also covers data breaches that occur as a result of theft. If a device is stolen, we immediately notify law enforcement so they can launch an investigation in the matter and will ensure that you're notified of any progress along the way. ERI takes great pride in doing everything possible to prevent data breaches and we have never been impacted by a data breach. However, should a data breach occur, we're prepared to handle it as quickly and efficiently as possible.

While it might seem like this type of data destruction is only beneficial to businesses, that's far from true. Everyone needs to be destroying their electronics with the same levels of precision. The rise of the Internet of Things has led to electronic data being stored on more devices. This means that everyone needs to be smarter in how they dispose of devices and everything needs to be destroyed. Men and women on the street wearing Fitbits need secure data destruction, both small and large corporations need data destruction, sensitive industries need data destruction, every branch in the federal government needs data destruction—*everyone* needs data destruction. The implications that we've covered in this book of poor data destruction are simply not worth it; the risk is too high. Find a recycling company that meets the standards and criteria we've discussed in this chapter and use them for every single piece of electronic equipment you need to dispose of.

Everyone knows that your phone, computer, and tablets have sensitive data that need to be properly disposed of. However, there are so many devices that carry data that many people don't even think about. To clear up any doubts, here is the start of a comprehensive list of devices that needs to be destroyed. Remember that both hard copies and soft copies of information should be destroyed.

- Phones—cell phones, smartphones, and landlines
- PDAs
- Laptops
- Desktop Computers
- Tablets
- Cameras
- Plotters
- Computer Monitors
- Televisions and Monitors
- Hard Drives / Solid State Drives
- USB Flash Drives
- USB Removable Media
- Firewall
- Floppy Disks
- Magnetic Disks
- Memory Cards
- Embedded Flash Memory on Boards and Devices
- Any Other Hard Copy Storage Device
- Scanners
- Modems

- Routers & Switches—from home, home office, and enterprises
- Servers
- Receivers
- Bridges
- Wearable Devices
- Reel and Cassette Tapes
- Optical Media (CD, DVD, Blu-ray)
- Cassettes
- VHS Tapes
- Reel-to-Reel Tapes
- Swipe and PIN Cards
- ID Cards
- Printers
- Photocopiers
- Fax Machines
- Projectors
- Circuit Boards
- Magnetic Tape Cartridges
- Multifunction Machines
- DATs
- LTOs
- ATA Hard Disk Drives
- ATA Solid State Drives (SSDs)
- SCSI Hard Disk Drives
- SCSI Solid State Drives (SSSDs)
- NVM Express SSDs
- RAM and ROM-Based Storage Devices

As we mentioned, we don't want to use this information as a way to get new clients to ERI specifically, but it's important to understand the difference between a reputable, trustworthy recycling company and a recycling company that could jeopardize your sensitive information. While it might cost a little more to use a recycling company that has all of the qualifications we've discussed, it's 100% worth it when you consider the alternative. Your personal data is invaluable and if it gets in the wrong hands, it will end up costing you far more than a few dollars here and there. Opting for hardware data destruction that protects your privacy is the only way to stay safe in a world that's becoming more and more digital every day.

Chapter 19: The Future of Privacy and Hardware Data Protection and Some Final Thoughts

In the midst of battling a major pandemic, 2020 and 2021 still managed to give us a glimpse into the future of technology, the Internet of Things, and how the trends of GDPR and 5G are going to converge. As we continue into the 21st century, we're hoping to see all of these trends finally find symbiosis with the migration towards a circular economy, more attention to cybersecurity, and a better outlook for responsible hardware destruction and electronic waste disposal. While we've experienced a lot of transformative revelations over the past decade, we believe we're only in the top of the second inning. We're still working towards our greater mission, but it's more exciting than ever because all of these trends are starting to come together to create a huge opportunity that could help make the world a better place.

Major institutions are becoming more transparent with how they use consumer data, which is going to open up competitive markets and new legislation for data security. The more that we know and understand, the more we'll realize how our data is used, sold, or put at risk when operating on third party applications or using smart devices. Legislation is being passed to better protect our data and how it's used by institutions. With the introduction of The Designing Accounting Safeguards to Help Broader Oversight Regulations on Data (DASHBOARD) Act, consumers are starting to see hope for a more level playing field.[1] The DASHBOARD Act requires companies to regularly disclose to consumers the ways in which their data are being used, the third parties it's being shared with, and what their data is worth on the platform.[1] From here, consumers will be able to decide whether or not they want to continue allowing institutions to access their data and will give them specialized access if they want to delete any or all fields of data that has been collected on them. This migration towards transparency is extremely important, especially when we look at the potential dangers of an unregulated surveillance state.

In China's technologically driven society, the government uses the Internet of Things to create a surveillance state and monitor their citizens. In the West, we too, are migrating towards a surveillance state. The primary difference between the two is the absence of any real regulation that recognizes the stakes at hand.[2] The U.S.'s surveillance state is emerging through corporations and consumer products, not government entities.[2] This creates a need for more privacy laws, better regulation of how our data is used, a need for proper hardware destruction and stronger data protection.

While the rapid expansion of the Internet of Things and 5G is going to make data protection more difficult, we can be more prepared by choosing responsible recyclers, increasing cybersecurity measures, and understanding the consent we give to our technology-integrated devices.

Since one of the biggest things that we'll see as we move toward 2030 is the switchover from 4G to 5G, we're also going to see an immense increase in hardware disposal. Many 5G operators will no longer work on 4G devices and will require an upgrade to the newest technology. This means that now, more than ever, we need to ensure that we're disposing our electronics properly. When we don't, we put ourselves at risk for cyberattacks, identity theft, and worse.

While there is still a lot of legislation in the process of being approved and turned into state and federal law, it's important to do what you can to make sure that your data and your clients' data is protected. One of the best ways to do this is to have a comprehensive list of resources that you can use as a reference point for future decisions, fact checks, and any services you may need. Throughout this book, our goal was to help educate the public regarding the dangers of cyberattacks on both software and hardware, the increasing impact of electronic waste on the environment and our security, and the shortcomings of our current laws.

As we continue to migrate to an increasingly digital world, we gain the benefit of accessibility and convenience, but we lose the security of everything. Now, more than ever, we need to do our due diligence and fully understand the implications of our technology. To help get you started, we've compiled a resource guide that includes more information on some of the top cybersecurity resources alongside ERI services, clients/industries, as well as some pertinent contact information. We hope that this book has given you direction in how to protect your data, the data of your clients, and reduce the environmental impact of your technology use in everyday life.

- Sustainable Electronics Recycling International (SERI) - https://sustainableelectronics.org/
- SERI's R2 Standard Certification - https://sustainableelectronics.org/r2-standard
- e-Stewards Certification - http://e-stewards.org/
- The National Association for Information Destruction (NAID) - https://naidonline.org/
- The International Organization for Standardization (ISO) - https://www.iso.org/home.html
- National Institute of Standards and Technology (NIST) - https://www.nist.gov/
- The Sys-Admin, Audit, Network and Security Institute (SANS) - https://www.sans.org/

- Global Information Assurance Certification (GIAC) - https://www.giac.org/
- National Initiative for Cybersecurity Careers and Studies (NICCS) - https://niccs.us-cert.gov/
- The NICE Cybersecurity Workforce Framework - https://niccs.us-cert.gov/workforce-development/cyber-security-workforce-framework
- Cybersecurity Workforce Development Toolkit - https://niccs.us-cert.gov/sites/default/files/documents/pdf/cybersecurity_workforce_development_toolkit.pdf?trackDocs=cybersecurity_workforce_development_toolkit.pdf
- Cybersecurity Workforce Planning Diagnostic PDF - https://niccs.us-cert.gov/sites/default/files/documents/pdf/cybersecurity%20workforce%20planning%20diagnostic_1.pdf?trackDocs=cybersecurity%20workforce%20planning%20diagnostic_1.pdf
- The NICCS Education and Training Catalog - https://niccs.us-cert.gov/training/search
- Cybrary - https://www.cybrary.it/
- Station X - https://www.stationx.net/
- STOP. THINK. CONNECT.™ - https://www.stopthinkconnect.org/
- Health IT Security - https://healthitsecurity.com/
- HIPAA Journal - https://www.hipaajournal.com/
- General Data Protection Regulation (GDPR) - https://gdpr-info.eu/
- Federal Trade Commission (FTC) - https://www.ftc.gov/
- The Department of Homeland Security (DHS) - https://www.dhs.gov/
- ZD Net - https://www.zdnet.com/

To learn more about the services ERI offers, please visit our website at https://eridirect.com. We proudly offer 100% responsible electronic waste recycling services that ensure your data is protected and destroyed.

- IT & Electronics Asset Disposition (ITAD)
- Data Center Decommissioning
- Data Destruction
- Electronics Recycling (E-Recycling)
- Secure Recycling Boxes
- Remarketing
- Logistics
- Redeployment
- Specialty Programs for Institutions

Sources – Chapter 1:

1. https://hypertextbook.com/facts/2002/BogusiaGrzywac.shtml

2. https://www.pewresearch.org/global/2019/02/05/smartphone-ownership-is-growing-rapidly-around-the-world-but-not-always-equally/

3. https://www.apartmenttherapy.com/how-many-tvs-is-too-many-tvs-158173

4. https://www.theatlantic.com/technology/archive/2012/01/the-new-laws-of-tv-upgrading/250998/

5. https://www.cnbc.com/2019/05/17/smartphone-users-are-waiting-longer-before-upgrading-heres-why.html

6. https://www.foxnews.com/tech/electronic-waste-pileup-sparks-warnings

7. https://www.theverge.com/2016/6/22/11991440/eri-e-waste-electronics-recycling-nyc-gadget-trash

8. https://resource-recycling.com/recycling/2019/11/15/in-our-opinion-collaboration-will-fuel-recyclings-evolution/

9. https://www.globenewswire.com/news-release/2019/09/19/1918300/0/en/New-Study-Shows-Recycling-Industry-Continues-to-be-a-Powerful-Force-in-U-S-Economy.html

Sources – Chapter 2:

1. https://www.wired.com/story/since-chinas-ban-recycling-in-the-us-has-gone-up-in-flames/

2. https://www.digitaltrends.com/cool-tech/e-waste-recycling-united-states/

3. https://resource-recycling.com/e-scrap/2019/01/31/stone-castle-ceo-sentenced-to-prison/

4. https://www.marketwatch.com/press-release/personally-identifiable-information-found-on-40-percent-of-used-devices-in-largest-study-to-date-2017-03-24

5. https://www.recyclingtoday.com/article/total-reclaim-fraud-ewaste/
6. https://www.chicagotribune.com/business/ct-biz-electronics-recycling-fraud-brundage-sentence-20190410-story.html
7. https://www.waste360.com/legislation-regulation/california-recycler-fined-mishandling-hazardous-waste
8. https://resource-recycling.com/e-scrap/2020/07/23/former-crt-firm-leaders-and-bank-face-fraud-accusations/
9. https://www.appknox.com/blog/cost-of-a-data-breach

Sources – Chapter 3:

1. https://www.securitymagazine.com/articles/87787-hackers-attack-every-39-seconds
2. https://www.dhs.gov/topic/cybersecurity
3. https://www.blackstratus.com/the-history-of-data-security/
4. https://www.clarip.com/data-privacy/us-history/
5. https://allpointsprotects.com/resources/what-is-naid-aaa/
6. https://naidonline.org/
7. https://www.csoonline.com/article/2130877/the-biggest-data-breaches-of-the-21st-century.html
8. https://www.healthcareitnews.com/news/employee-error-exposed-data-16000-blue-cross-patients-online-3-months
9. https://www.welivesecurity.com/2019/06/24/nasa-breach-mars-raspberry-pi/

Sources – Chapter 4:

1. https://www.ellenmacarthurfoundation.org/circular-economy/concept
2. https://www.activesustainability.com/sustainable-development/what-is-circular-economy/
3. https://reports.weforum.org/toward-the-circular-economy-accelerating-the-scale-up-across-global-supply-chains/from-linear-to-circular-accelerating-a-proven-concept/

4. https://www.europarl.europa.eu/news/en/headlines/economy/
20151201STO05603/circular-economy-definition-
importance-and-benefits

5. https://www.circle-economy.com/circular-economy/7-key-
elements

6. https://www.fastcompany.com/90300741/most-u-s-
companies-say-they-are-planning-to-transition-to-a-circular-
economy

7. https://corostrandberg.com/wp-content/uploads/2016/11/hp-
and-the-circular-economy.pdf

Sources – Chapter 5:

1. https://www.gdpreu.org/the-regulation/who-must-comply/

2. https://www.darkreading.com/edge/theedge/5-pieces-of-
gdpr-advice-for-teams-without-privacy-compliance-
staff/b/d-id/1336651

3. https://www.gdpreu.org/the-regulation/timeline/

4. https://www.gdpreu.org/

5. https://www.forbes.com/sites/andrewrossow/2018/05/25/the-
birth-of-gdpr-what-is-it-and-what-you-need-to-know/

6. https://www.theverge.com/2018/5/25/17393766/facebook-
google-gdpr-lawsuit-max-schrems-europe

7. https://www.zdnet.com/article/gdpr-an-executive-guide-to-
what-you-need-to-know/

8. https://gdpr.eu/what-is-gdpr/

9. https://www.theverge.com/2019/7/12/20692253/facebook-
ftc-settlement-fine-5-billion-justice-department

10. https://www.forbes.com/sites/jillgoldsmith/2019/01/21/franc
e-slaps-google-with-e50m-fine-for-privacy-violation-under-
gdpr/

11. https://www.siliconrepublic.com/companies/salesforce-
oracle-cookies-gdpr

Sources – Chapter 6:

1. https://www.forbes.com/sites/jillgoldsmith/2019/01/21/franc e-slaps-google-with-e50m-fine-for-privacy-violation-under-gdpr
2. https://www.theverge.com/2019/7/12/20692253/facebook-ftc-settlement-fine-5-billion-justice-department
3. https://www.red-gate.com/simple-talk/sysadmin/data-protection-and-privacy/gdpr-in-the-usa/
4. https://www.darkreading.com/edge/theedge/5-pieces-of-gdpr-advice-for-teams-without-privacy-compliance-staff/b/d-id/1336651
5. https://blog.netwrix.com/2019/08/27/data-privacy-laws-by-state-the-u-s-approach-to-privacy-protection
6. https://iapp.org/resources/article/state-comparison-table/
7. https://www.ncsl.org/research/telecommunications-and-information-technology/consumer-data-privacy.aspx
8. https://www.congress.gov/bill/116th-congress/senate-bill/189
9. https://www.congress.gov/bill/116th-congress/senate-bill/142/
10. https://www.congress.gov/bill/116th-congress/house-bill/2545
11. https://www.congress.gov/bill/116th-congress/senate-bill/2968/text
12. https://www.congress.gov/bill/116th-congress/senate-bill/2961/text
13. https://www.congress.gov/bill/116th-congress/senate-bill/3663
14. https://www.rokhanna.com/issues/internet-bill-rights

Sources – Chapter 7:

1. https://www.forbes.com/sites/jacobmorgan/2014/05/13/simple-explanation-internet-things-that-anyone-can-understand/
2. https://www.zdnet.com/article/what-is-the-internet-of-things-everything-you-need-to-know-about-the-iot-right-now/
3. https://www.fastcompany.com/90291265/reminder-all-those-smart-devices-are-a-growing-security-threat
4. https://www.kait8.com/2019/12/12/cyber-security-expert-gives-safety-tips-home-security-cameras/
5. https://www.wsj.com/articles/cyber-protections-lag-behind-growth-in-connected-devices-11575887401
6. https://www.techrepublic.com/article/63-of-organizations-face-security-breaches-due-to-hardware-vulnerabilities/
7. https://www.usatoday.com/story/money/cars/driveon/2019/02/06/your-car-might-hackable-heres-what-cybersecurity-experts-say/2777300002/
8. https://techcrunch.com/2019/12/01/fbi-smart-tv-security/

Sources – Chapter 8:

1. https://www.wsj.com/articles/the-rise-of-the-smart-city-1492395120
2. https://blogs-images.forbes.com/jacobmorgan/files/2014/05/libelium_smart_world_infographic_big.jpg
3. https://www.wsj.com/articles/the-rise-of-the-smart-city-1492395120
4. https://www.zdnet.com/article/what-is-the-internet-of-things-everything-you-need-to-know-about-the-iot-right-now/
5. https://constructech.com/the-rise-of-smart-cities-and-the-impact-on-construction/
6. https://www.wsj.com/articles/smart-cities-will-require-smarter-cybersecurity-11568107802

7. https://www.natlawreview.com/article/cybersecurity-and-electric-grid-new-gao-report-identifies-actions-needed-to-address

Sources – Chapter 9:

1. https://www.forbes.com/sites/moorinsights/2017/09/25/your-datacenter-is-not-safe/
2. https://www.techrepublic.com/article/cyberattacks-now-cost-businesses-an-average-of-1-1m/
3. https://www.npr.org/2019/01/11/684610280/hacks-are-getting-so-common-that-companies-are-turning-to-cyber-insurance
4. https://techhq.com/2019/11/redundant-hardware-proving-a-data-risk-for-businesses/
5. https://www.techrepublic.com/article/63-of-organizations-face-security-breaches-due-to-hardware-vulnerabilities/
6. https://www.infosecurity-magazine.com/news/used-drives-sold-sensitive-data-1-1/
7. https://www.pcmag.com/news/many-used-hard-drives-sold-on-ebay-still-contain-leftover-data
8. http://www.pbs.org/frontlineworld/stories/ghana804/video/video_index.html
9. https://its.ucsc.edu/security/breaches.html
10. https://www.marketwatch.com/press-release/personally-identifiable-information-found-on-40-percent-of-used-devices-in-largest-study-to-date-2017-03-24
11. https://fortune.com/2019/06/26/federal-cybersecurity-48-year-old-system/
12. https://scholarship.law.duke.edu/cgi/viewcontent.cgi?article=1319&=&context=dltr
13. https://cybersecurityventures.com/internet-of-things-hacks/

Sources – Chapter 10:

1. https://fortune.com/2019/02/21/technology-companies-federal-data-privacy-law/
2. https://www.fifthdomain.com/dod/army/2019/08/29/how-one-teenager-took-out-a-secure-pentagon-file-sharing-site/
3. https://fortune.com/2019/06/26/federal-cybersecurity-48-year-old-system/
4. https://www.bloomberg.com/news/features/2018-10-04/the-big-hack-how-china-used-a-tiny-chip-to-infiltrate-america-s-top-companies
5. https://www.wired.com/story/supply-chain-hacks-cybersecurity-worst-case-scenario/
6. https://www.nytimes.com/2019/02/18/technology/hackers-chinese-iran-usa.html
7. https://gizmodo.com/usb-drive-found-on-jailed-mar-a-lago-party-crasher-cont-1833893988
8. https://www.nytimes.com/2013/03/19/us/disposal-of-older-monitors-leaves-a-hazardous-trail.html
9. https://www.nytimes.com/2020/03/17/world/europe/germany-missile-laptop.html
10. https://www.businessinsider.com/western-countries-send-servers-full-of-sensitive-information-to-foreign-countries-2018-12
11. https://www.nytimes.com/interactive/2019/04/10/opinion/internet-data-privacy.html
12. https://www.digitaltrends.com/cool-tech/e-waste-recycling-united-states/

Sources – Chapter 11:

1. https://www.paubox.com/blog/what-is-hipaa
2. https://digitalguardian.com/blog/what-hipaa-compliance
3. https://www.hhs.gov/hipaa/for-professionals/privacy/index.html

4. https://www.bleepingcomputer.com/news/security/over-38-million-healthcare-records-exposed-in-breaches-over-2019/

5. https://www.telegraph.co.uk/news/0/cyber-crime-warning-experts-say-hackers-deliberately-target/

6. https://healthitsecurity.com/news/data-of-15m-patients-impacted-retrieved-in-lifelabs-cyberattack

7. https://healthitsecurity.com/news/rsa-keys-found-in-iot-medical-devices-implants-prone-to-attack

8. https://www.wsj.com/articles/behind-googles-project-nightingale-a-health-data-gold-mine-of-50-million-patients-11573571867

9. https://www.healthcareitnews.com/news/when-medical-devices-get-hacked-hospitals-often-dont-know-it

10. https://ryortho.com/breaking/victims-can-sue-ortho-clinics-if-data-hacked/

11. https://deloitte.wsj.com/cio/2019/12/17/protect-iot-data-in-the-health-ecosystem/

12. https://gizmodo.com/medical-files-of-145-000-vulnerable-rehab-patients-care-1834177125

13. https://www.telegraph.co.uk/news/0/cyber-crime-warning-experts-say-hackers-deliberately-target/

14. https://www.csoonline.com/article/3249765/what-is-the-dark-web-how-to-access-it-and-what-youll-find.html

15. https://www.modernhealthcare.com/cybersecurity/november-reported-healthcare-breaches-exposed-570000-patients-data

16. https://deloitte.wsj.com/cio/2019/12/17/protect-iot-data-in-the-health-ecosystem/

17. https://bc.ctvnews.ca/privacy-breach-at-medical-lab-could-affect-millions-in-b-c-ontario-1.4733926

18. https://healthitsecurity.com/news/oig-finds-ineffective-data-network-security-at-hhs-fda-cms-nih

19. https://techcrunch.com/2019/12/10/healthcare-focused-venture-firms-are-forming-a-best-practices-group-for-securing-health-data/

20. https://www.healthdatamanagement.com/list/10-critical-steps-in-the-safe-disposal-of-data-devices
21. https://www.hipaajournal.com/mercy-health-discovers-phi-of-978-patients-was-exposed/
22. https://healthitsecurity.com/news/the-10-biggest-healthcare-data-breaches-of-2019-so-far
23. https://wwjnewsradio.radio.com/articles/news/beaumont-data-breach-exposes-sensitive-information

Sources – Chapter 12:

1. https://www.fdic.gov/regulations/compliance/manual/8/viii-3.1.pdf
2. https://www.hitachi-systems-security.com/blog/data-security-regulations-overview-by-industry-finance/
3. https://www.ftc.gov/tips-advice/business-center/privacy-and-security/gramm-leach-bliley-act
4. https://www.ftc.gov/enforcement/rules/rulemaking-regulatory-reform-proceedings/safeguards-rule
5. https://www.consumer.ftc.gov/articles/pdf-0096-fair-credit-reporting-act.pdf
6. https://www.ftc.gov/enforcement/statutes/fair-accurate-credit-transactions-act-2003
7. https://www.ngdata.com/data-privacy-guide-for-banks-and-financial-institutions/
8. https://www.capgemini.com/wp-content/uploads/2017/07/Data_Privacy_in_the_Financial_Se rvices_Industry.pdf
9. https://www.tcs.com/content/dam/tcs-bancs/protected-pdf/Understanding-Data-Privacy-in-the-Financial-Services-World.pdf
10. https://techcrunch.com/2019/01/23/financial-files/
11. https://www.nytimes.com/2019/07/19/business/equifax-data-breach-settlement.html

12. https://www.ftc.gov/news-events/blogs/business-blog/2019/07/575-million-equifax-settlement-illustrates-security-basics

13. https://www.nytimes.com/2018/04/19/business/wells-fargo-cfpb-penalty.html

14. https://www.pcmag.com/news/capital-one-breached-100-million-customers-affected

15. https://www.nytimes.com/2019/04/10/opinion/insurance-ai.html

16. https://www.wiley.law/alert-FTC_Announces_Proposed_Changes_to_Cybersecurity_Regulation_for_Financial_Institutions

17. https://www.cfr.org/report/reforming-us-approach-data-protection

18. https://www.capgemini.com/wp-content/uploads/2017/07/Data_Privacy_in_the_Financial_Services_Industry.pdf

19. https://www.onespan.com/blog/top-banking-regulations-security-compliance-requirements

20. https://www.upguard.com/blog/new-york-cybersecurity-regulations-explained

21. https://www.jdsupra.com/legalnews/vermont-adopts-new-information-privacy-82812/

22. https://www.ciodive.com/news/62-of-breached-data-came-from-financial-services-in-2019/569592/

23. https://gizmodo.com/885-million-sensitive-records-leaked-online-bank-trans-1835016235

Sources – Chapter 13:

1. https://www.retaildive.com/news/us-retailers-lead-world-in-data-breaches/528873/

2. https://www.bloomberg.com/news/articles/2017-11-21/uber-concealed-cyberattack-that-exposed-57-million-people-s-data

3. https://www.fastcompany.com/90324748/supreme-court-rejects-amazons-zappos-on-data-breach-lawsuit

4. https://www.retaildive.com/news/data-thieves-go-after-adidas-other-sports-and-fitness-sites/527018/

5. https://www.databreachtoday.com/wendys-reaches-50-million-breach-settlement-banks-a-12032

6. https://techcrunch.com/2019/11/19/macys-said-hackers-stole-customer-credit-cards-again/

7. https://legalnewsline.com/stories/511787747-chicago-sues-marriott-over-data-breach-claiming-hotel-chain-failed-to-protect-personal-information

8. https://www.wsj.com/articles/accenture-faces-lawsuit-over-marriott-data-breach-11565343001

9. https://www.retaildive.com/news/tis-the-season-for-retail-security-threats/510084/

10. https://www.cybergrx.com/resources/research-and-insights/blog/the-latest-retail-breaches-third-party-data-breaches

11. https://upserve.com/restaurant-insider/pos-data-breaches/

Sources – Chapter 14:

1. https://www.zdnet.com/article/us-military-purchased-32-8m-worth-of-electronics-with-known-security-risks/

2. https://www.defenseone.com/ideas/2018/01/time-get-serious-about-hardware-cybersecurity/145210/

3. https://www.nextgov.com/cybersecurity/2019/02/navy-needs-2-tons-storage-devices-burned-ash/154629/

4. https://www.vice.com/en_us/article/7xy5ky/the-american-military-sucks-at-cybersecurity

5. https://www.nbcnews.com/tech/security/opm-hack-security-breach-n389476

6. https://www.militarytimes.com/news/your-military/2018/10/12/pentagon-reveals-cyber-breach-of-travel-records/

7. https://www.military.com/daily-news/2020/02/25/dod-agency-suffers-data-breach-potentially-compromising-ssns.html

8. https://www.nbcnews.com/tech/security/dod-communications-hub-reports-likely-data-breach-n1140071

9. https://www.forbes.com/sites/daveywinder/2020/02/21/us-defense-agency-that-secures-trumps-communications-confirms-data-breach/

Sources – Chapter 15:

1. https://www.cnbc.com/2019/02/05/your-car-might-be-easier-to-hack-than-you-may-think.html

2. https://www.usatoday.com/story/money/cars/driveon/2019/02/06/your-car-might-hackable-heres-what-cybersecurity-experts-say/2777300002/

3. https://www.nytimes.com/2019/03/07/business/car-hacks-cybersecurity-safety.html

4. https://www.cnbc.com/2019/03/29/tesla-model-3-keeps-data-like-crash-videos-location-phone-contacts.html

5. https://www.criticalhit.net/technology/a-tesla-3-hack-shows-massive-amounts-of-unencrypted-data-stored-in-the-car/

6. https://www.vice.com/en_us/article/zmpx4x/hacker-monitor-cars-kill-engine-gps-tracking-apps

7. https://www.techrepublic.com/article/hackers-finding-ways-to-exploit-automotive-software-to-overtake-cars/

8. https://www.washingtonpost.com/technology/2019/12/17/what-does-your-car-know-about-you-we-hacked-chevy-find-out/
9. https://gb.mitsubishielectric.com/sites/gb/en/news-events/releases/global/2019/0122-b/index.html
10. https://www.automotiveisac.com/
11. https://www.wsj.com/articles/european-regulators-propose-privacy-security-rules-for-connected-car-data-11582799402

Sources – Chapter 16:

1. https://www.tomsguide.com/us/5g-release-date,review-5063.html
2. https://www.adweek.com/digital/the-shift-from-4g-to-5g-will-change-just-about-everything/
3. https://www.abiresearch.com/press/5g-silver-bullet-smartphones-will-necessitate-refreshed-vendor-strategies-arrest-declining-market-growth/
4. https://www.wsj.com/articles/from-wi-fi-to-bluetooth-to-5g-all-your-wireless-is-about-to-change-11548597600
5. https://www.zdnet.com/article/5g-points-the-way-to-life-beyond-the-smartphone/
6. https://www.adweek.com/digital/all-the-5g-phones-and-rollout-dates-announced-at-this-weeks-mobile-world-congress/
7. https://www.cnbc.com/2019/04/03/verizon-begins-rolling-out-its-5g-wireless-network-for-smartphones.html
8. https://www.androidcentral.com/5g-us-how-each-carrier-will-deploy-5g-phones
9. https://www.fastcompany.com/90334146/the-trump-administration-will-unveil-major-5g-initiatives-today
10. https://www.fcc.gov/auction/904

11. https://www.benton.org/blog/what-rural-digital-opportunity-fund
12. https://www.allconnect.com/blog/fcc-5g-fast-plan-for-rural-connectivity
13. https://nymag.com/intelligencer/2019/02/5g-is-going-to-transform-smartphones-eventually.html
14. https://www.zdnet.com/article/how-5g-can-help-unlock-iots-potential/
15. https://www.darkreading.com/mobile/security-top-concern-as-mobile-providers-think-5g/d/d-id/1334620
16. https://www.ft.com/content/74edc076-ca6f-11e9-af46-b09e8bfe60c0

Sources – Chapter 17:

1. https://nvlpubs.nist.gov/nistpubs/SpecialPublications/NIST.SP.800-46r2.pdf
2. https://www.fastcompany.com/90446916/four-ways-remote-workers-can-prevent-security-breaches
3. https://www.techradar.com/news/remote-working-is-leading-to-a-rise-in-data-breaches
4. https://www.itproportal.com/news/remote-working-leading-to-more-data-breaches/
5. https://www.forbes.com/sites/carrierubinstein/2020/04/10/beware-remote-work-involves-these-3-cyber-security-risks/
6. https://www.identityforce.com/business-blog/remote-workers-data-breach
7. https://www.fifthdomain.com/civilian/dhs/2020/04/08/dhs-releases-new-network-security-guidance-for-telework/
8. https://www.zdnet.com/article/the-remote-working-rush-is-creating-a-playground-for-spies-and-cybercrooks/

9. https://www.zdnet.com/article/ransomware-and-ddos-attacks-cybercrooks-are-stepping-up-their-activities-in-the-midst-of-coronavirus/

10. https://www.zdnet.com/article/fbi-says-cybercrime-reports-quadrupled-during-covid-19-pandemic/

11. http://spaceref.com/news/viewsr.html?pid=53512

12. https://cisomag.eccouncil.org/cybercrime-will-cost-the-world-us6-trillion-by-the-end-of-the-year-study/

Sources – Chapter 18:

1. https://www.prnewswire.com/news-releases/personally-identifiable-information-found-on-40-percent-of-used-devices-in-largest-study-to-date-300429076.html

Sources – Chapter 19:

1. https://www.scribd.com/document/414097487/Dashboard-Act-1-Pager

2. https://www.nytimes.com/interactive/2019/04/10/opinion/internet-data-privacy.html

Made in the USA
Columbia, SC
23 July 2021